D1599077

Laughter and the Love of Friends

Martin Cyril D'Arcy, S.J.

Laughter and the Love of Friends

Reminiscences of the
Distinguished English Priest and Philosopher

Martin Cyril D'Arcy, S.J.

Collated and Edited By
William S. Abell

CHRISTIAN CLASSICS, INC.
Post Office Box 30
Westminster, Maryland 21158
1991

FIRST PUBLISHED 1991
© 1991 BY THE BRITISH PROVINCE OF THE SOCIETY OF JESUS

ISBN: 0 87061 189 5
LIBRARY OF CONGRESS CARD CATALOG NUMBER: 91-73299

PRINTED IN THE USA

From quiet homes and first beginning,
Out to the undiscovered ends,
There's nothing worth the wear of winning,
But laughter and the love of friends.

Dedicatory Ode
Hilaire Belloc

Table of Contents

Preface xi

Foreword..xv

The D'Arcy Family..1

Early Schooling...5

Stonyhurst...9

Noviceship...13

Oxford..23

Theology...35

Campion Hall..45

Modernism...59

Early Jesuit Friends...83

Belloc, Chesterton and Baring 105

Some Other Friends...127

Oxford Again...145

Heroic Figures...163

A Group of Eccentrics..179

Inspiring Stories 189

Strange Stories...197

Illustrations

1. Father Martin C. D'Arcy............................Frontispiece

2. Stonyhurst College.....................................Facing pg. 9

3. Augustus John portrait of Fr. D'Arcy........Facing pg. 42

4. Campion Hall...Facing pg. 45

5. Farm Street Church.................................Facing pg. 99

Preface

In the fall of 1960, Father Martin D'Arcy, S.J., was in residence at Georgetown University while he delivered a series
of lectures to philosophy students. Father Edward Bunn,
S.J., then President of the University, brought Father
D'Arcy to dinner at our home in Chevy Chase one October
evening, and our relationship developed so pleasantly that he
became a relatively frequent guest at our table. His charming
personality, marvelous conversation and delightful sense of
humor made those evenings most enchanting.

At that time I was reading *Felix Frankfurter Reminisces*,
a book put out by Columbia University as a byproduct of the
University's program of recording comments and observa-
tions on the contemporary scene by a limited number of
public figures. The purpose was to develop archival material
for future writers. I was impressed with the Frankfurter
book and developed the idea of taping some of Father
D'Arcy's recollections. I had found his table talk most interesting and conceived his comments on English literary and
academic figures, mostly Catholic, to be matters worth pre-
serving for students of the first few decades of the twentieth
century.

At first, Father D'Arcy was reluctant, but in the end he
yielded to my importunities. For some six or eight Monday
evenings over the course of the winter, he joined us for dinner and I undertook to record his comments on selected per-

sons and subjects. In the end I found myself with a number of tapes, but, due to my poor recording techniques, all quite difficult to decipher and reduce to the typewritten page. However, my wife and I managed to do this and, further, succeeded in getting Father D'Arcy himself to edit the material. He gave me permission to publish all or part of the text, subject only to my keeping the English Province posted in advance on what I planned to do.

Professional and business pressures kept me away from the project for several years and then I read that Father D'Arcy had appeared on TV in England and had apparently discussed much of what I had recorded. I seized this information as an excuse to do nothing. Recently, however, I ran across the text and also chanced to spend some time in London and to make a number of visits to Farm Street Church. Suddenly it seemed important to me that those reminiscences of Father D'Arcy be made available to the public.

Out of respect and affection for Father D'Arcy I urge readers to keep in mind that these are reminiscences, and not statements based upon research. They should therefore be read as parts of conversations, and allowances should be made for faults of memory on the part of this gentle, intellectual, interesting and charming man.

Also, I think it important to mention that the early chapters, relating to the D'Arcy family and to Father D'Arcy's personal life, did not come until the very end of our recordings. At that time, I pointed out that some personal background information on him would be helpful to anyone reading his reminiscences. Only at my urging, and with some reluctance on his part, did he speak about those early days of his life. It was my decision that proper sequence should put those chapters at the beginning of the text. The words are, of course, still those of Father D'Arcy.

From the winter of 1960–61, to Father D'Arcy's death in 1976, my wife and I kept in close contact with him and saw him frequently, both in our house here in the United States and in London as well. Out of these many associations with him we formed a clear impression of a remarkable man. He had a brilliant mind, a superb education. He had contributed to theological and philosophical thinking. He was a perfect gentleman, possessed of a kindness, gentleness and sensitivity only too infrequently encountered. He had a keen sense of humor and a delightful laugh. His was an engaging personality, and he could and did meet individuals of all levels of society with equal ease. Despite his own brilliance, perception and established position as an outstanding intellectual, he had a genuine interest in the views of others and an ability to show respect for their opinions. A man of refined taste, he had a love for the beauty of the world, be it natural or man-made—art, architecture, literature or science. His great humility and personal holiness were apparent to anyone who knew him well. But perhaps the facet of Father D'Arcy which was most unusual and moving to me was the spontaneity and ease with which he spoke of Christ. He was the only person it has been my privilege to know who would frequently refer to "my beloved Jesus" in a personal, tender, totally unaffected and moving manner. Father Martin Cyril D'Arcy was a lovely man, and it was a privilege to know him as a friend.

I wish to acknowledge my debt to my wife, Patricia, for heroic service in the entire project of this book, but especially for those delightful dinners in the early days and, later, for assistance in translating my poorly recorded tapes to the point where they could be typed. My son, W. Shepherdson Abell, has earned my gratitude for his constant encouragement and for his considerable contributions once the decision was reached to move forward to publication. I am indebted to Cindy Farley and to Judy Cooney for their splendid work in typing the manuscript. I also extend my thanks to Dr. Joseph Jeffs, former librarian of Georgetown University's Lauinger Library.

September 1991   *William S. Abell*

Foreword

Martin Cyril D'Arcy was born in Bath, England, on June 15, 1888, the son of a distinguished Catholic lawyer. The family was of Irish and Norman descent.

He attended Stonyhurst College, the senior Jesuit college in England. When he left the college at age eighteen he entered the Jesuit novitiate at Roehampton. In 1912 he was sent to the Jesuit hall at Oxford to seek a degree. He earned a Second in Classics, and followed it two years later with a First in "Greats." His academic success was brilliant. He won the Charles Oldham Prize while still at Oxford and subsequently received two other important University awards, the John Locke Scholarship (1918) and the Green Moral Philosophy Prize (1923).

After leaving Oxford he returned to Stonyhurst to teach for three years. His methods and personality were especially effective in individual tutorials and with small groups of students. In 1919 he entered upon his theological studies and was ordained in 1921. The year 1923–24 was spent at Stonyhurst on a special teaching project. He took his tertianship in Ireland and was then sent to Rome to the Gregorian University to do doctoral work in philosophy.

After two years of study in Rome, Father D'Arcy was returned to Oxford, where he began to lecture in philosophy. In 1933 he became Master of the Jesuit college in Oxford. When the college was moved to its present location, he retained the services of Sir Edwin Lutyens, the leading English architect of the day, who designed Campion Hall, a building of singular architectural beauty. Father D'Arcy's personal contribution to the artistry of the Hall was his collection of works of sacred art, especially paintings, sculptures, vestments and chalices. The end result was a gem, Campion Hall becoming, on a small scale, one of the more aesthetically attractive colleges of the University.

In 1936 Father D'Arcy made the first of his many visits to the United States. On one such trip during the early stages of World War II, he found himself interned in America for a considerable period before he could return to Oxford. It was during this wartime period that he began what ultimately became an ancillary career of lecturing at American universities. Over the years he lectured at Boston College, Columbia, Cornell, Fordham, Georgetown, Loyola (Baltimore), Loyola (Chicago), Minnesota, Notre Dame, Princeton, the University of California, Wesleyan, Yale, and other educational institutions. It is interesting to note that there is now a Martin D'Arcy Gallery of Art at Loyola in Chicago.

In 1945 Father D'Arcy was appointed Provincial of the English Province. His period at this post produced mixed results. He had a wide vision and an imaginative eye for Jesuit opportunities. He showed rather a romantic compulsion to purchase for Province use old houses with historic Catholic associations. He also had a plan for the establishment of a unique college of education in the Leeds area which came to naught because he failed to secure the support of the local bishop. While he was a superb and devoted superior, deeply and effectively considerate of the men for whom he was responsible, he was something less than a successful administrator.

A poor delegator of authority, he insisted upon handling too many details and was impatient of bureaucratic paperwork. Moreover, he neglected the formalities of informing or consulting with bishops about enterprises he was contemplating in their dioceses. Even more critically, he was inadequate in his communications with Rome. This type of administration of the Province met with disfavor. The end result was that, after five years, he was rather abruptly removed from the post of Provincial in 1950. There was consternation among his peers in the Order, and he had the sympathy of virtually every Jesuit in the Province. It had apparently been a case of an extremely talented person placed in the wrong position. It was a traumatic experience for a very sensitive man. The curtailment of his term of office left him with a deep sense of failure. But Father D'Arcy quietly accepted the situation and continued with his life as an obedient Jesuit. Officially he remained a member of the Farm Street Church staff in London, but he was left a free agent and pursued his scholarship, his writing, his preaching, his lectures and his almost annual visits to the United States.

From his early days at Campion Hall through his period as Provincial, Father D'Arcy made a considerable impact upon a variety of circles in Oxford and in London. He had a wide acquaintance in both places. Outstanding academics of every type were frequent guests in the common room at Campion Hall when he was Master there. His dinners in London were celebrated and memorable. Interesting and articulate guests from academia, the arts and the political scene were at his table. He was a splendid host and a fine orchestrator of intelligent and amusing conversation.

Father D'Arcy wrote extensively, producing more than a dozen books, including *Pain and the Providence of God, The Mass and The Redemption, The Spirit of Charity, The Nature of Belief, Mirage and Truth, The Problem of Evil, The Mind and Heart of Love, The Matter and Meaning of History.* However, the consensus appears to be that he was not a natural or born writer and not at his best in his writings. They demonstrated no compelling style, were not often simple and clear, but very cerebral and difficult to read. A certain eloquence and warmth showed through but they did not carry the charisma of the man himself. Only too little of his own simple and ardent personality and spirituality was evidenced. His books failed to do him justice.

Father Martin D'Arcy was a man of slight, wiry figure. With his hair carefully combed almost like a crest, bristling eyebrows and flashing eyes, his appearance immediately attracted attention. He had a charismatic presence, a flame-like quality. Quick of movement, he spoke with great animation. Abundant gestures, constantly changing facial expressions, nodding head, darting eyes, he was all motion. There was something almost birdlike about him. He had a splendid sense of humor and was quick to smile and laugh. His whole appearance was an attractive and compelling one, and in his quiet way he dominated most scenes upon which he entered.

A man of great intellectual energy and passionate convictions, he was a fascinating conversationalist, a superb raconteur, a master at introducing and guiding discussions. He had a remarkable ability for drawing out the thoughts of others and showing respect for their opinions.

Father D'Arcy was an extremely sensitive person and exercised great tact in his relations with people. He was a careful respecter of the privacy of others and expected the same from them. While he sometimes enjoyed teasing, he was always careful not to injure feelings. He was kind by nature, thoughtful of others, courteous and beautifully mannered. With a mind that was always eagerly inquiring, he delighted in spirited discussions.

He had a highly romantic view of the past and was very much a royalist at heart. Moreover, unashamedly an elitist, he delighted in the company of persons of recognized social, literary, scientific and religious rank. A subtle but effective apologist, he was proud of being a Catholic intellectual and ever quietly demonstrated his deep and conservative Catholicism.

Father D'Arcy was a remarkable man, endowed with many gifts. A complicated person, he had a life which was not without contradictions. He achieved many great successes but also suffered telling failures. As we saw, he fell short of gaining a First in Classical Moderations at Oxford, but was spurred by that experience to earn a First in "Greats" and to win important Oxford prizes. He greatly enjoyed the company of persons of the upper level of English society and English intellectuals. The conversation at his Campion Hall dinners and those he later hosted in London was stimulating, witty and learned, the food and wine of the best. The events were always great successes. Father D'Arcy himself was somewhat ascetic in his personal habits and would partake only lightly of the menu at his dinners. He thrived more on the conversation and the personalities of his guests. The selection of those at his table demonstrated his interest in and his respect for individuality, even eccentricity. There were those who regarded him as a snob, but the charge was baseless. He was just as fully at ease with persons at the upper and the lower levels of society and was himself a distinctly humble man.

In the field of philosophy he was open to modern intellectual currents but unmoved by them. Although some scholars regarded him as retrogressive, others held him to be one of the eminent philosophers of his day. His books are not generally regarded as significant contributions to philosophical thinking. However, several of his theological works were held in high esteem. Surely he was a superb apologist and one of the most persuasive voices of Catholicism in England. He was in the mould of the Christian humanist, and confidently and passionately defended and fostered the truest of human values. He delighted in maintaining contact with students and was always interested in the ever-changing intellectual currents of youth.

Martin D'Arcy was at his best in personal relations. As a counsellor he was magnificent, his perception, understanding, and sympathy enabling him to give very helpful advice. His retreats and talks to other small groups, such as graduate seminars, were uniformly successful. He was not always an effective public speaker, but occasionally his brilliance and intensity would deeply move an audience—even as sophisticated and normally restrained an audience as a group of Oxford academics.

He deeply loved the Jesuit Order and was held in affection by the members of the English Province. His deposition as Provincial was the severest of blows, one from which he never fully recovered. But the deep regard he held for the Order and his fellow Jesuits made Farm Street the home to which he always returned. The death of this wonderful human being and truly holy man left a void in the Jesuit community, as it did among his friends outside the Order throughout the world.

Father D'Arcy died on November 20, 1976. His health had failed during that year and his death came as no surprise. He himself had in fact come to look forward to the end. A Requiem Mass was celebrated in Farm Street Church, Cardinal Hume being the principal celebrant. Father Frederick Copleston, the well-known Jesuit historian of philosophy and a one-time student of Father D'Arcy's at Campion Hall, preached. Another Requiem was later celebrated at Oxford, where a close friend, Lord Hailsham, delivered the eulogy. Father D'Arcy was buried in the Jesuit burial grounds of Green. R.I.P.

The D'Arcy Family

My family was the Norman branch of the D'Arcys, who ultimately settled in Ireland. But during the Cromwellian period they were driven out of their places near Dublin, and out to Roscommon, where they had a large estate. They were, of course, always Catholic.

My grandfather was supposed to have been the handsomest man of his time. I have a number of photographs of him, and they do make him look extraordinarily fine. He was a tall man, about six feet two, most aristocratic and fierce, but with a violent temper. I remember my father (who absolutely adored my grandfather) telling me that once when he and his wife were in a railroad carriage in Ireland, a man got in with a pipe in his mouth. So my grandfather said, "I'd be glad if you put that pipe out, sir." Well, the man paid no attention, and my grandfather thereupon took one smack at the pipe, sent it sailing out of the window, and said, "Perhaps you'll stop smoking now, sir."

The family story is that my grandfather drove in to Dublin as a young man at about the time the Shelbourne Hotel had just been founded by a family named Burke, from Dalkey. My grandfather saw the daughter of the family, they fell in love with each other, and he took her off and married her. His relatives felt he had married beneath himself, and they were furious. As a result he got absolutely on the outs with them and wouldn't have anything to do with them at all. That's where much of his trouble started. I remember my father telling me that he went over to Kingstown (it's now Dun Laoghaire) and somebody was talking to him and boasting about some family, you see, and my father said, "Oh, they're nothing at all. They're nothing to a D'Arcy." And the man said, "On your father's side, none better; but your mother was born on the rocks of Dalkey." Actually, I'm told that the Burkes were a quite good family.

My father was a barrister. He came over from Ireland and practiced in London for a time, then went off to act as political agent for Lord Bath in Somerset. There were three famous families who were supposed to have succeeded in seizing vast monastery lands at the time of the Reformation. One was the Horners, the second was the Pophams, and the third was a family called Thynne. The Horners retained the best of the properties (supposedly the plum of the Jack-Horner-sat-in-a-corner story). Some distance off is the Thynne property. The original Thynne became a great Whig aristocrat and had one of those enormous houses down in Piccadilly that figure in novels of that period and part of the world. They were a very good-looking family and married quite well. They gradually worked up to be barons, and the head of the family became the Marquis of Bath. Well, the son of the Lord Bath of my father's day wanted to stand for

Parliament. The old man himself was in the House of Lords and his son was anxious to stand in the House of Commons until he succeeded his father. But there were mining villages in that part of the country and so he had to fight for his seat. My father acted as his political agent. Father was a silent type and didn't talk much about himself, but every now and then he would tell me, when I was a child in Bath, of how he used to fight those campaigns. Sometimes he had to drive back a whole mob of rough, stone-throwing miners, just with a stick. These miners were liberals, strongly anti-conservative. Lord Bath, on the other hand, represented all the conservative and reactionary elements to these mining groups that were coming up just at that period. So my father, as political agent for Bath, sometimes had quite literally to fight these miners.

I think that old Lord Bath finally quarreled with my father, accusing him (as I remember) of trying to make a political career of his own. The story goes that my father turned to him and ordered him out of the room, and that ended his career as political agent at Bath. It was after this incident that my father resumed his practice of the law and joined the Northern Circuit as a barrister. That's how I came to go on to Stonyhurst, you see.

Early Schooling

There had been four children in our family, but two died young, and so there were really only my elder brother and myself. My very early schooling was in the area of Bath. I was sent to a small prep school called Freshfield when I was only about eight years old (very young, but that was the habit in those days). I can remember singing for joy most of the way to school the first day. Then when my mother and father left me, I cried my heart out, of course.

While I own that the home is the greatest of all places in the world for children, I do think there's a good deal to be said for sending boys off to boarding school at fourteen or so. But before that, I must own, I think it's very debatable indeed. I survived, but it was pretty grim. I remember my second day at school: the priest there, who was a wonderful man and knew my father, came round and comforted me. I was smallish for my age and so frightened meeting all these bigger boys. I suppose they weren't so big really, but they looked dreadfully big to me.

I remember early on I went out for a walk with another little freshman boy. Now in my father's library there were many volumes of *Boxiana* which I knew almost by heart.

You see, I had started to read very early. This may sound like boasting, but I don't intend it that way. It's only for a comparison with what so often I find now to be the case with boys. They just don't seem to read. By the time I was about twelve I had read a lot of Scott, I had read a then well-known series of wonderful stories about the fall of Rome, I had read novel after novel. I had seen pictures of Dante's *Inferno*, and so on. At any rate, the day this tiny boy and I went for a walk together I spent the whole afternoon telling him of my prizefighting. Right out of the *Boxiana*! I put the stories in the first person, you see. To this day I still don't know whether I was telling lies or whether it was childish imagination.

Later I went to Hodder, the Jesuit preparatory school for Stonyhurst. It's only about a mile from Stonyhurst itself. I used to hate the life there. My, how I hated it! The school was very rough and there really was a struggle for existence. There was an awful lot of bullying in those days. I remember that to keep one brute of a boy from turning his satellites on me, I had to go and buy tea for him and his friends over the longest time. I'd buy cakes and things, and thus dispense my narrow means just to keep me safe from the others.

It was supposed to be a very nice school, but those were hard days. No heating, and one was all chilblains. You were turned out of doors each day, no matter what the weather was. But you certainly learned a lot. You went into the schoolroom simply terrified. You were given, shall we say, twenty or thirty lines of English poetry and thirty lines of

Latin—your Caesar or whatever it was, you see. When you went to class, the Master would say, "D'Arcy, by heart." If you missed a single word or even faltered, he'd order "a dozen." That meant a dozen cracks with a kind of gutta-percha, leather weapon, about the size of your thumb, called a ferula. You were never punished by the same person who ordered the "dozen." It was the prefects who actually administered the punishment. There were certain hours when you were supposed to go down and into this particular room; there would be a man there, and he'd say, "You've got a dozen. Hold out your hand." I couldn't stick that. Those were rough days, they really were. Most of the boys were big, strong, healthy fellows and they just took it in their stride. They didn't seem to mind it a bit.

When I was at Hodder, there were epic tales told of a dreadful Australian bully who was in the school at Stonyhurst. He was pointed out when we went up from Hodder to High Mass. (We used to go up to the college to plays and to High Masses.) This boy's face looked exactly like leather, and he was supposed to be an absolutely fearless bully. The poor boys sitting next to him at table! He would just fill up their glasses with mustard and any filthy stuff he could pick up, and would say, "Drink it. Go on, drink it!" Apparently, at one stage a fine, handsome Irish boy named Mullin got fed up with this and tore into him. And we heard of an epic struggle in which they had fought off and on for three days behind the handball court. And Mullin had absolutely smashed him, you see.

7

In those days there was an enormous study hall with about two or three hundred desks in it. Each desk had about sixty or seventy brass names attached to it, listing the boys who had sat there and going back for generations and generations. When you were a new, small boy, you were right up under the prefect; then you gradually moved back, you see. But I remember a big fellow named Barry, a big Irish boy who was about six feet tall. He was always in trouble, so they moved him up just under the prefect. But then you'd see him sauntering into the hall after breakfast with his hands in his pockets, just having had "twice nines," and he'd lean back and yawn and look insolently up at the prefect.

Then there was a small area just near the lavatories where all the fights would take place. You'd be going to the lavatory after supper, and in this darkened space, with only some dim light from the gas jet, you'd see two of the boys having a terrific fight. Everyone would crowd around them and watch to the end. But things were changing even then, and conditions gradually became more tolerable. When I first went to Stonyhurst they'd just changed from beer at four o'clock, and I don't think I had any meat at all for the first three or four years there.

There was an awfully nice priest at Hodder who was a marvelous gamester, and at cricket he could make the ball break from one corner to another. I think he was drawn to me, I don't know quite why. At any rate, he always saw that I was brought some porridge for breakfast. That may have been one reason why I so adored him.

Stonyhurst College

Stonyhurst

From Hodder I went up to Stonyhurst, where the Jesuit Order maintains a junior school and junior college of about five hundred boys. I loved the place, despite many hardships, and I suppose I did fairly well in my classes. I won a lot of prizes, but I was always beaten by one or two people in final standing.

The history of Stonyhurst is rather interesting. It was a large private property during the Tudor times, and the oldest part of the present structure was built in the days of Queen Elizabeth by a Catholic family called Shireburn. Then they died out, I think, and the estate passed into the hands of the Weld family. The Welds already had many properties, and for a long period they rather neglected this one. At this period, owing to the French Revolution, the great school of St. Omer's, to which parents of English Catholic boys had sent their sons for generations, closed down. About that same time the Jesuits had a chance to come back to England and they were looking around for a location. Well, Thomas Weld offered them this place in the north near Manchester. The Jesuit fathers arrived there around 1794, built a temporary house, and gradually added on to it. Finally they repaired the old manor house and made it into the magnificent building you see today. Then, about 1880, Father Purbrick—who was a very capable man and, incidentally, one of the Oxford converts—added enormous and majestic buildings on to the property. Almost the whole of the English Province was centered there in those days.

I can still remember my days there and many of the boys who were with me. For example, I can recall a boy named Leicester. He was a very thin, sandy-haired youngster, and he always finished sentences perfectly. He couldn't play games at all, had no dexterity whatsoever. So he was mercilessly bullied. They'd say, "Give me your food, Leicester. Oh, you won't?" and push him under the table. Well, this Leicester came from a very large family that lived in Worcester. They'd been chartered accountants for generations. Leicester's father was Mayor of Worcester. When the First World War broke out, Leicester joined the army and rose to be a major. At one point he created a tremendous stir because, in the training maneuvers, orders were issued to attack Worcester and put a force into it. Apparently Philip Leicester was in charge of the attacking force. And he just walked clean into Worcester! He told me afterwards that it was very simple: Oliver Cromwell had captured Worcester in the seventeenth century, so Leicester looked up and studied the campaign very carefully and just used it over again.

Despite everything he endured, Leicester has today a passionate love of Stonyhurst. Passionate! What all of us came to enjoy when we finally got to the top was tremendous. The bullying was really a dying thing by then; when we reached the top, I don't think we did any bullying at all. And we had come to love the place so! We all were crying, I remember, when the last day—Academy Day—came. It was terribly sad.

I myself wanted to be a lay philosopher. There were only two places in the Society of Jesus which had this course, Feldkirch and Stonyhurst. Owing to the fact that Catholics weren't allowed to go to Oxford and Cambridge until 1896, the Jesuits had put in this course of two years of philosophy. At Stonyhurst these particular students all had rooms looking out on the great avenue which went for half a mile with trees on both sides—extremely beautiful.

These lay philosophers came not only from Stonyhurst but from other schools as well. The course became more and more aristocratic because people like the great South American families wanted to get a touch of English education for their sons and would send them to this philosophy course; the great Spanish nobility came there, and Catholic boys from other schools in England; some of the Hapsburgs were there.

You really had the time of your life. You had your room all to yourself, absolutely to yourself. You smoked just as you liked (in those days in most public schools in England you'd be expelled immediately for smoking). You played golf. You fished. You could hunt. You could do anything you wished, and the only punishment was a form of fine if you didn't attend classes. I have a very pleasant memory of it all.

When I went down, I suppose there were about forty lay philosophers. They didn't mix with the boys in the school, you see. It was a kind of school within a school. They had their own records and chapel, everything. You had classes, but they were small classes. Several of the boys would be going in for higher examinations and they'd come there to be coached. There was a man from Beaumont, one or two from Downside; there were even two or three from the United States—one from Fordham, as a matter of fact. I still remember that particular boy. His father and his uncles had all been at Stonyhurst and then had scattered over the world. His father was now in the United States, and the boy had been going to Fordham. I remember asking him, "Where do you come from?" And he said, "From Fordham." And I asked, "Where's that?" So he answered, "It's in New York." And I asked, "What kind of place is it?" "Oh, very like this. About three hundred boys there." When I went back to Fordham in 1940 there were about seven thousand, I would say. More now, of course.

Noviceship

After Stonyhurst I reached the decision to enter the Order and immediately went on to noviceship. Among my most vivid memories is the occasion when my life was saved by a wonderful medical diagnosis. I was in my second year as a novice and had been put in charge of outdoor work in the gardens. Well, one day I began to feel very unwell, running a high temperature. They put me to bed and said I had got the flu. So this flu progressed and I began to have a really very high fever, about 105°, for several days. The doctor tried me for typhoid and for everything else he could think of, but he couldn't find out what was wrong. So then they told me, "You're dying. There's no question about it. You'll probably die tonight." Well, when you're a novice in a religious order, I suppose they feel they should tell you outright like that. But I can still remember my nature saying, "No, I'm not going to die."

Whatever my spiritual desires to go to heaven might have been, there was this tremendous, terrific impulse to live. So vividly did I remember this impulse that afterwards, when as a priest I'd go around hospitals making visits, I'd use presence or absence of it as a standard (not always valid, of course) to tell who were really dying and who were not. At any rate, it seemed to me you could see a look on certain faces that they felt it was all over. They were dying. Then you'd see other people who were supposed to be dying, but still the struggle was not over, their nature hadn't given in.

In this illness of my noviceship, my own nature hadn't given in at all. I felt that very strongly myself. You see, all novices are bent on being unselfish, and yet I had this extraordinary feeling of self coming on. It was rather puzzling to one: the last fight, as it were.

I can still remember all sorts of interesting things about those twilight days. How at that period I hated the person who came just to dilly-dally, and wasn't of any use to me. The effort to be polite and nice to such people was of a supernatural order. But when a person came in who could do something for me, that was something else again. I can recall the night I was told I would probably die. They brought in a great old country doctor, with enormous experience, a really first-class man in his own right. I can remember his entering my room, top hat still on his head, and saying, "Well, that boy looks no good. Mmm." Then he started doing the usual things, checking me here and there. Now, during this illness there'd grown up a swelling on my left arm, and this old doctor suddenly said, "How did you get that scratch on your thumb? Huh! What this boy's got is blood-poisoning. That's what's happened. The blood-poisoning has spread up here now, where the swelling is. He'll die probably. He's very far gone. But better get us a specialist in." So then they

14

brought in the specialist and he recommended an operation, and I lived. Otherwise I would not be here now. But there's a case of what I call the old-fashioned, real medical diagnosis.

You know, when a man looks back on life, he wonders why his experiences have not made a more lasting impression on him. When the window glass in my room broke in recently during a storm, it gave me very much more of a shakeup than normally it would have, owing to the fact that I had had a near-fatal accident once when a porthole blew in on me aboard ship and very nearly killed me. And so the breaking of the window pane was this reinforced experience of a thing out of the past suddenly become alive again.

When I was in the novitiate, Father Daniel Considine was the Master of Novices. He was a Jesuit of whom I have lovely memories. He came from a great Irish family. His brother was the head of the Royal Irish Constabulary, and the family were all brilliant gamesters. A little story I know about the brother is that when his children would go off to a dance or some other social event, he would not infrequently show up there on his horse and say, "Come on, come home now. You've had your merriment. Now you must give glory to God. We'll have the rosary first, and then we'll have night prayers."

Daniel Considine was at Stonyhurst and then he went on to Oxford. This was before Oxford was really open to Catholics, but Catholics "dropped in," and Father Considine, having proved to be something of a scholar, was sent there. Then, being a very holy man, a man of enormous sanctity, he was put on as Master of Novices at Roehampton, and there he remained for many years. Physically he was smallish in size, but with a great leonine head. He had a magnificent way of speaking and showed a very dry sense of humor. He was exceedingly generous—the kind of man to take off his coat and give it to the first poor man he'd meet, you see, and then have to look about for another coat for himself. He did not write very much, but some two or three works of his were published posthumously. In them he showed deep spirituality, and they have been an enormous help to many people, I think. *Words of Comfort* was one of them.

But apart from his holiness, I would think the most notable of Father Daniel Considine's characteristics was his tremendous power of self-control. Let me give you an illustration of his control. The novitiate dining room at Roehampton was perhaps twenty yards long, and there were novices on each side of the table, with Father Considine, the Rector, at the head. Well, on this occasion it was summertime and the wasps were buzzing about, you see. One of the novices took a napkin and flapped it around, and the wasps flew off. To our amazement (novices were supposed to "keep custody of the eyes"), we saw a wasp settle on Father Considine's face; but he made not the slightest movement, and for quite some minutes the wasp moved about on his face undisturbed. So when we got to recreation after dinner, I turned to a fellow novice and said, "Brother, did you see what hap-

pened to Father Master? That's a lesson in control to us."
And his only reply was: "I was praying the wasp would
sting him."

Sometimes this imperturbability even bordered on a kind
of bravery. When he was Master of Novices and Rector, he
admitted a Polish boy to Roehampton. And apparently this
boy began to go cracky. One day he came in from the far end
of the dining room and began in a most menacing manner to
roll up the length of the room towards Father Considine,
who was standing there waiting for grace to be said. The
Master saw him coming up, looked at him quite sternly and
firmly waved him back. There was a pause during which the
boy glared at the Rector, and then he turned and slowly went
back to his place. And when the Master came down, this
poor demented boy spat in his face and threatened him; but
Father Considine was absolutely calm and unmoved, and
spoke gently in an effort to soothe him. Such imperturbability and self-control was absolutely amazing, and provided
a great lesson to all the novices who passed through Roehampton while Father Considine was there. But Father must
have sensed that this boy was in a very dangerous condition,
for he was put into a room with two husky lay brother
novices to watch after him.

About one o'clock one morning, he went raving mad and
started making noises, roaring and shouting and pitching
things at these two brothers, and they skedaddled out of the
room. Well, the roaring and thrashing about continued and
there was a gathering of people outside the door. Among

them there was a German Jesuit father who was a very great man at Fordham afterwards—an authority on ants or something like that. He suggested that they should have a blanket, throw the door in and rush at this boy with the blanket, get it over him and hold him down. He was raving mad. All over the novices' quarters you could hear him roaring like a bull. It was terribly frightening. Well, they did as the German father suggested and they got him down. Then Father Considine was brought along, and the poor boy spat at him as Father tried to soothe him. When they tried to tie the boy up, he broke his ropes and ran into beautiful Richmond Park just outside the novitiate, and they had to run after him and catch him and bring him back. Well, I was in the great corridor of the building, one side of which was all glass; and as I was walking along, suddenly I heard noises, looked out the window, and there they were putting him in to a horse-drawn cab which had been brought by the asylum authorities. As I watched, they put him in one side and he broke through the other, and his face suddenly turned right at mine—and he glared at me and snarled like an animal. I couldn't get that picture out of my mind for a long time. It remained with me for years, awful and depressing. Those are examples of impressions of youth. They stay with you in a way, but just how much do they really affect you?

You get back to the problem: what does unbalance a personality? A while ago we were talking about my early days at school. So many people now would say the roughness and the harshness that we went through must have created all sorts of complexes. But it didn't, on the whole, and the question is: why not? Why did relatively few boys of my generation show any really apparent effects? And in the generations before, they must have gone through infinitely more, because I lived in a relatively humane age when I was a child. You wonder how they could have stood it. And you think of what people have just recently gone through in prison camps during World War II and Korea. Yet many of those have survived in their whole personality. I believe that the ones who did so were the ones who, first of all, had the background against which to make their judgments.

When Father Considine ceased to be Master of Novices at Roehampton, he was made Rector at Wimbledon. Then he was pushed off to Farm Street, because in the old days they always had a holy man there, and Father Considine was the one in his day, you see. Then he developed a disease which finally made him completely cracky—Bright's disease, I think it was. For quite a period before his death, he took to giving "advice" in a strange sort of way. There was a very sentimental Spiritual Father up at Stonyhurst at the time, and this man used to send a list of boys to what he called "the holy old man"—that is, Father Considine—to find out whether they had vocations. And Daniel Considine would come back with a classification for each name. It must have been a period when his mind was failing, you see, because I can't conceive of the man I had known as Master of Novices doing anything like that. It must have been the effect of his disease. Though he had become rather cracky, fellow Jesuits

19

and others would still come to see him and talk with him. One day after such a session, he turned to the brother who was looking after him and said, "Brother, it's very humiliating to talk nonsense and be aware of it."

Certainly he was very holy. Before he died he was supposed to have been raised in ecstasy at Mass. Again, I've heard a brother say that, upon entering Father Considine's room, he saw him all bathed in light. He was, indeed, a remarkable man, and I had a profound admiration for him.

Somehow I am reminded of a book by Pamela Johnson, the wife of C.P. Snow. It is obviously written around that fantastic figure, Frederick Rolfe, Baron Corvo, although she places the character in her book in Bruges instead of in Venice. Well, this man of enormous pride gets himself invited out to dinner. Now, he's been living in absolute poverty, with nothing to eat, so that his stomach has greatly contracted. And here is all this delicious food before him, and he realizes very quickly that it's going to make him sick because his stomach is out of the practice of digesting! (That's a thing you can apply to the spiritual order, too, but it is forgotten constantly.)

I've seen people, as they get older in the Society of Jesus, become more and more dyspeptic and fussy about their stomach and their foods. Why? Because they've been cutting themselves off and living on the simplest possible foods. As a result, after a time their stomachs simply can't handle anything they take outside these habitual foods.

It is a great theory of mine that if you want really to keep your health, you mustn't live a very bread-and-butter life in the community and then expect to go out someplace and eat a splendid dinner. Because if you've been living on bread and butter, your stomach will tell itself that's all it wants. It's no longer exercising itself and struggling for existence, grappling with strange, different foods. The thing is to keep your body and your stomach in a condition in which they've got an activity to perform, some fight, a kind of struggle for existence. As long as you do that, your nature will generally rise to the occasion. But if you surrender, then you will find, after about a year or two, that you've lost the power of eating decent food or of drinking wine.

I remember an article by a very brilliant man who claimed that the whole secret of living is to have resistances. An eagle cannot fly unless it's got air to resist, wings to flap against it. Our stomachs are really made to eat brontosaurian stuff, to eat reindeer meat and the rest. We're finished when we live on finer foods. No wonder all the troubles with the human stomach. Lots of women have given up the struggle to have children, and therefore they can't have them even when they want them. I think there's an extraordinary power in nature in that way. Give nature a chance, and it will overcome obstacles. Let it not fight, and its powers to fight die. So, too, even with childbirth.

Oxford

It was my great good fortune to be sent up to Oxford after I had done my philosophy. Not many years earlier this would have been an impossibility. Pope Leo XIII was the one who gave leave for Catholics—but only an occasional Catholic under specified conditions—to go to Oxford or to Cambridge. He did so after Cardinal Manning's death when Cardinal Vaughan, the brother of Father Bernard Vaughan, came on. At that time the Catholics of England, headed by the Duke of Norfolk, urged the Cardinal to ask Rome for the necessary leave. To his great credit, although he had been a disciple of Manning's, he petitioned Rome, and, about 1896, Pope Leo XIII gave leave for Catholics to go to Oxford and Cambridge under certain conditions. One was that there should be a Catholic chaplain; another, that there should be conferences given on Catholic topics. (That explains why occasionally you still come across books in old libraries entitled *Oxford and Cambridge Conferences*.) Now, there was a statute of Oxford that an M.A. Oxon. of good repute could petition the University for leave to open a private hall, which would be called by his name but would cease to exist when he withdrew or died. Well, a number of

Oxford men who became converts in those days had ultimately joined the Jesuits; and one of them—a very distinguished man—was Father Richard Clarke, who wrote a book on logic and a Stonyhurst series on other subjects. He'd been a Fellow, one of the dons of St. John's College. He'd been a rowing "blue," too. We still have his oar at Campion Hall. So he petitioned the University and, sure enough, they granted the petition, and that started Clarke's Hall. Two of our scholastics had got first class honors at London University, so we decided to send these two to begin our career at Oxford.

When I was a small boy at Stonyhurst, in the program at the great academies they used to list the school's great awards and successes from the past. I used to gaze with absolute marvel at Father Joseph Rickaby, "First in all England" in this, that and the other, and at Father Peter Gradwell, gold medal for one thing or another. And I said to myself, "My goodness, these Jesuits have obviously been the best in the whole of England!" In my simplicity what I didn't realize until much later was that in those days these Jesuits got external degrees at London University, and if they sent a person in for philosophy, there would probably be only about six different candidates, and it wasn't quite so very distinguished when he finished on top! But it seemed tremendous to a schoolboy when he saw "First in all England."

Well, Oxford had gone far ahead of any other place in England for scholarship (Cambridge men to the contrary notwithstanding!). The Jesuits were therefore very wise when they took these two scholastics who had already got first honors in London, and sent them to Oxford as the original Jesuits at the University. After another four years of hard work, one of them succeeded in getting first class honors and the other got a second. That's how the Jesuits got started at Oxford.

Then the Benedictines from Ampleforth followed suit. They had a most distinguished convert named Hunter Blair who was an Oxford man. (They used to joke about him and call him the Abbot of Tours because he was always traveling about the world. He'd been at Magdalen with Oscar Wilde and was well known as Sir David Hunter Blair, Bart. before he became a Benedictine.) So he started the Benedictine Hall at Oxford. Now, they had had two top boys at Ampleforth School who had decided to be Benedictines. So they thought they'd send these two boys and their master (this story was told to me afterwards by one of them) as their first students at the University. They arrived in Oxford and shortly went off to see their tutor. He saw that one of the three was much older than the others, so he turned to him and said, "You intend to take honors, do you? Tell me what you've read in the way of Latin and Greek." The master started to list what he'd read, and the two boys sat in wondering admiration. When he'd finished, the don said, "Ummm. You really intend to take honors? I'm afraid you've read so little. I strongly advise you to take just a pass degree." Well, the master and the two boys were ready to climb under the table!

Which shows the wisdom, the astuteness of the Jesuits in, as I say, having chosen two men who already had degrees as their original students at Oxford. At any rate, that's how the first two Catholic halls were started.

The Jesuit Hall began very luckily. At that time there were in the Society a group of very remarkable young men. That's one of the mysterious happenings in life: how things seem to go in groups. I don't quite understand it. It has occurred frequently at Oxford. (This is a digression, but when I went back to Oxford after ordination to teach there before I became master, there was an extraordinarily brilliant group of undergraduates: W.H. Auden, Stephen Spender, Day-Lewis and men of that stature. There were poets, and there were novelists; there were men who are now among the leading politicians in Great Britain, and they were all there together. Then there come pauses in which you don't hear about anybody very interesting, and then another exciting set comes in. They seem to infect each other and become twice as clever as even they had been before.)

Well, there was a group of this type of young men in the Society just when Clarke's Hall was founded. There were C.C. Martindale, Charles Plater, a Father Lattey, who was a great scripture scholar in the Catholic world of his time, and one or two great mathematicians. So they gave the Hall a magnificent start, you see. But even so, it was terribly difficult in those early days. While we thought some of our young Jesuits were pretty good, they often would start out at Oxford tremendously handicapped. They would be pitted against the absolutely brilliant boys coming out from those top public schools, boys who had been coached individually by great scholars. It was quite something to see a mere boy come up and just put his feet on the mantelpiece and read Greek and Latin like they were novels.

I still remember as an undergraduate, walking along the Turl, a very narrow medieval street in Oxford, with a Jewish boy named Victor Gollancz. He has since become a leading English book publisher and has written his autobiography. I understand that he's a Christian now. At any rate, we had just been to a lecture by one of the great Latin scholars of the world, so that Latin was very much on my mind. And I said to this boy, "The examination is drawing near. Are you worried?" And he answered, "No, I don't give much thought to the examination these days. You see, I'm going to try out for some of the very highest prizes. I was working hard last night until midnight. Then I got bored and tired of reading and working, and so I took to turning the prophet Malachi into Lucretian hexameters." I was a bit skeptical about this, so I asked, "Did you really? Have you got them on you?" He was carrying a pile of volumes; so he set them down, looked through them and finally came up with some sheets of paper, saying, "Yes, here we are." And there it was—a beautiful set of Lucretian verses. Well, Lucretius has a rare Latin style, a rather primitive style. It was somewhat like saying, "I'll turn this poem into Chaucerian English." Yet this young boy could do that at midnight, just as a recreation. So, you see, we were struggling against a pretty high standard in those days.

I had gone up to Oxford after my philosophy course. That was one of the requirements insisted upon by Rome: you had to do your philosophy before you went up to the universities. But our limited scholastics' knowledge of philosophy didn't stand up against the professors of philosophy at Oxford. Not because the philosophy itself wasn't better, of course. But after all, if you have a man who has rushed through a three-year course of metaphysics, logic, psychology and all the rest, and then you suddenly put him up against one of the best minds in the world, one which has been dwelling upon philosophical matters for forty years, well, he's not going to just carry the day.

There was an astonishingly fine set of thinkers in those days at Oxford. And they were men of the highest rectitude. They wouldn't let you get away with anything except what was absolutely right and accurate. There was a marvelous cleansing of the mind, a mental spring-cleaning to be had from talking with them. I'll give you an example of what I mean.

I had a young friend at Oxford who thought of himself as rather a good writer. One day he went off to a tutor's conference with the famous H.W.B. Joseph, who was a positive mental magician, with an absolutely needle-sharp mind, deadly logical. Joseph had told my friend to treat of Mill's methods for his first essay, and I can still see him sitting back and stroking his head just before he left, using phrases like "great essay" and "worth publication." Well, he came back like a dog with his tail between his legs. As I recollect, the first sentence in this great essay began, "In the middle of the Victorian era the philosophical world was divided between empiricism and idealism." Evidently my friend read out that sentence, and Joseph said, "One moment. Would you just read that again?" So he read the sentence again, and Joseph said, " 'In the middle of the Victorian era...' What year were you thinking of?" Of course, my friend had not been thinking of any particular year, so he tried to start again. "The philosophical world..." but was interrupted again. "What precisely do you mean by that?" After about another twenty minutes, my friend was completely muddled: his words didn't seem to mean very much. Then Joseph showed him that he didn't know what either empiricism or idealism meant. He never got beyond that first sentence! Now, that I call excellent training for the mind.

I have said that the Oxford professors of my day were men of the highest rectitude. They were true gentlemen. Let me illustrate by telling you of something that actually happened to a young Jesuit friend of mine. He was a shy man, a very highly strung person, and so sensitive that if the word *blood* was mentioned in conversation, he would have to leave the room. This man was asked by the same H.W.B. Joseph to do an essay on free will. After he'd been struggling with the whole thing for a while, he finally settled on the three famous arguments of Father Michael Maher's book on psychology. So he did his essay and presented it. He started the first argument, and Joseph—again carried away by this passion for getting at exactly what was meant by words—asked questions which my friend wasn't able to answer. Then came the second argument, and the same thing happened; and the third argument, and Joseph, now enamored of the whole question, was pressing his advantage when he suddenly noticed the young man was desperately upset and on the verge of tears. To Joseph's great honor, when he saw this, he got very upset himself: "Oh, oh, oh... I beg your pardon. I beg your pardon. I never meant in any way to upset your beliefs. Oh, I do beg your pardon! Let us end now. Let us discuss this on some other occasion. I do beg your pardon!" Now, that shows a very good tradition, I think.

I was very lucky at Oxford, you see. I took a "First" in what is called "Greats." You take the humanities for about a year and a third; then you take what's called "Moderations," Latin and Greek, and take a pure Latin and Greek examination. If you get a first or second in that, you go on to "Greats" proper. There you study your Plato, your Aristotle, your Roman and Greek history, and, finally, all modern ideas in the light of that background. I was especially lucky because in the classics I had Robinson Ellis, who was then one of the three greatest Latin scholars in the world. When I went on to Greats, I had Toynbee for a term. I had a wonderful professor of Roman history who again ranked amongst the two or three great scholars of the world in that field. And in Greek history I had an extraordinary character, a clergyman who wrote articles in the *Encyclopaedia Britannica* on Greek History. His name was Walker. He was phenomenally learned and had a prodigious memory; moreover, he was an altogether delightful gentleman. He had special views of his own on Greek history, which at the time were the leading ones. I remember that one of the other Jesuits used to say it was apt to be a very trying ordeal to study under him because, in order to illustrate some point in Greek history, he would suddenly say, "Oh, of course, it's very like what your Jesuit Father Bellavada said in the year 1602 at Tokyo, in Japan," and even though you were a Jesuit yourself, you very likely had never heard of Father Bellavada! Walker would be able to give extraordinary examples all over the place. You never knew where his knowledge would stretch.

There was quite a famous story told of him. He was lunching with the Benedictines one day, and the Catholic chaplain of the University—who was a convert and who'd been out in Asia Minor as a clergyman—got vexed at Walker's prodigious knowledge. So he thought he would start a subject which would leave Walker without anything to say. He mentioned something about a tremendous rainfall at a place called Makarna (as I recall) in Asia Minor. Walker listened with that intense interest which he always showed and finally said, "Most interesting, Father, most interesting. What year was that?" And the chaplain said, "1903." "Well," said Walker, "I remember: I think it was in 1901 at Manarna—that's five (or is it six?) miles from Makarna—there

31

was a rainfall about a half inch greater than the one to which you refer." You can imagine where that left the chaplain! Walker was a wonderful and charming man, so well-disposed towards the Church, so understanding of it. Everybody loved him.

Then in philosophy I had the man I have always regarded as one of the greatest thinkers of the last one hundred years or so. That was Professor Cook-Wilson. Unfortunately he didn't publish much, but he was a tremendous thinker. (Some of his works were published posthumously.) Then I had Joachim, the renowned idealist thinker and the nephew of the great Hungarian violinist. And I had one or two others of the same caliber, so I was very lucky.

I'd like to tell you two stories about Oxford, both of which I enjoy beyond words because they are so Oxfordian and give something of the flavor of my beloved University. In 1914 or 1915, before World War I conscription came in, an undergraduate at Oxford was walking down the High when a woman confronted him, saying, "What are you doing here while your brothers are fighting for civilization?" He just looked at her and said, "Madam, I *am* the civilization they are fighting for."

The other story relates to an incident that happened only three or four years ago. It gave me such pleasure because it made me realize Oxford still goes on as it used to. A very brilliant undergraduate was taking Greats. After you've done your fortnight's papers (about ten or twelve papers, three hours each), you wait until the four examiners can go through them. Then, after about six weeks, you come back for an oral—or *viva voce,* as they call it. This oral may last only a few minutes, it may be an hour or it may go longer, depending on whether the examiners are quite satisfied. They already know your qualifications pretty well and have given you their mark on the papers. Well, in this case the examiners apparently thought that the young man was very brilliant, but they weren't quite sure of his depth, of how solid he was. So they put him through a long period of questioning. This went on and on—about an hour to an hour and a half, I suppose—but they could not bring him to heel. Finally, one of the examiners, rather exasperated, said, "Mr. X, will you kindly answer *yes* or *no* to that question?" And the boy said, "Well, if you put it that way, sir, I'd say *no,* but in the sense of *not yes.*" So the examiner said, "Ah, Mr. X, you admit then the notion of *not yes,* do you? You accept that concept?" "Well," said the boy slowly, "I *did,* sir!"

Did I ever tell you what occurred in my own case when I took my orals? It's quite unimportant, but it may be interesting to you. I went along on that morning with several other undergraduates and was waiting my turn in an awful state of trepidation. It's a very formidable thing, you know, these four men in cap and gown, and so much hanging on it from your point of view. Well, my name was finally called out. Then suddenly I heard, "No, it's a mistake; we'd like Mr. X, not you." So I sat down again. And this same thing of my name being called by mistake happened two or three times! It was most unusual and extremely upsetting. Finally my turn did come and I went in and sat down. One of the examiners looked up and said to me, "Ah, Mr. D'Arcy, I see in your paper that you refer to what is called *aevum*. It's not time, it's what the angels live in. Would you give me a further development of that idea of yours?" I was in such a state of nerves at this point that I could only say, "Oh, I'm afraid that it would be very difficult for me just now to try and develop that idea on the spur of the moment here. It's so abstruse. I'd like to have my text before me." "I understand," he said. "All right, Mr. D'Arcy, thank you. That's quite enough. Thank you. Good day." And I walked out. That was the only question I was asked, and that was my *viva voce*!

Theology

After Oxford came my theology. I spent my first year of theology with the French Jesuits at St. Leonard's-on-Sea. The Paris and Lyons Province—in fact, all the French Jesuits—had been exiled during those awful years at the beginning of the twentieth century. In the First World War they went back and forth between France and England in the ranks; then after the war, a law was passed allowing them back into France. So two or three years after I finished my studies at St. Leonard's, both they and the Jesuits from Jersey went back to France. But in my time they were still in exile.

They had at that time the very great and wonderful Père de Grandmaison, who wrote *The Life of Christ* and started so many great movements. They had Lebachellère and the magnificent Rousselot. In fact, a good case can be made that the French have carried the Church on their shoulders for practically the last seventy years. I'm always sorry that there's not more recognition of this. Just test it. Whatever you mention proves the point. Take scripture. A French Dominican, Père LaGrange, and Père Vincent were undoubtedly the two greatest scripture scholars who lived in this period. LaGrange wrote four great volumes on the evangelists, and Vincent wrote on the discoveries out in Palestine. Then you had Père Prat, who wrote a splendid book on Saint Paul, and Père Huby, who again wrote on that theme. Then on the mystical life you had a great Frenchman whose name escapes me for the moment. You had Rousselot in philosophy. In Belgium you had Père Charles and you had the man who wrote five volumes on the theory of knowledge. All in all, the French were marvelous at that time. The Belgians were very good, too.

At about the time I was finishing theology, the Provincial, who was a lovely Irish gentleman named Father Bodkin, came to do his visitation at the house of studies and he said to me, "Look here. Would you be prepared to go back to Stonyhurst and sacrifice a year? There are three very exceptional and interesting boys there who could profit greatly by studying with you." Then he named the boys: Henry John, Christopher Devlin and Thomas Burns. Well, I was rather complimented, though I really hadn't much interest in the project. In any event, I went back to Stonyhurst for the year and loved every minute of it. The three boys really did prove to be outstanding.

I was captivated by Henry John, that most brilliant son of Augustus John, the painter. He had the genius of his father, but in his case it turned to writing rather than painting. It was words, not paint that fascinated the son. He wrote his own history of India when he was seven years old. He could sit down and dash off quite beautiful poetry at the age of twelve or so. In many respects, he was an absolute genius.

Henry was the youngest of Augustus John's numerous progeny. I think his mother died either at his birth, or else very soon thereafter. The father, who had loved his wife very deeply, wasn't up to raising an infant, so he sent the child back to his grandmother. And there was a Miss Nettleship, a cousin, who eventually took the boy and brought him up. Later Augustus stole the child back, and then the good lady stole the child from him again. At least, so the story goes.

At any rate, Miss Nettleship took charge of the child. She was a nurse in the First World War and became a Catholic at that time; and although Henry wasn't a Catholic boy, she sent him to Stonyhurst. That's where I came into his life. After the Provincial had mentioned him to me, we got into correspondence. What letters this boy would write!

He became a Catholic when he was about fifteen. Then Frank Sheed came up to Stonyhurst, quite enthused about the Catholic Evidence Guild (on which he had worked very hard), and he suggested that the boys could do a bit of Guild work. Henry John welcomed the idea, and he went up to London and spoke frequently in Hyde Park at the age of about sixteen or seventeen. The result, of course, was devastating for the enemies of the faith. Here was this boy, handsome, looking like an angel (except he was dark), and with this wondrous power of words, this gift of oratory. The crowds left all the more famous speakers of the Protestant Alliances, the Jews and the Socialists, to gather round this child, to the absolute indignation of the enemies of religion. They'd say, "That child ought to be in bed!" One evening he spoke on miracles, and right at the end a voice was heard to say, "Miracles? That bloody boy is a bloody miracle himself!" It was incredible, it really was. And he was such a nice boy.

In his fervent convert days (he was only about sixteen), Henry once received some pamphlets from the Catholic Truth Society of Great Britain. One of them was on Saint Aloysius, and it carried a picture of Saint Aloysius wearing a surplice, holding a lily, and looking very pious. Well, Henry immediately wrote the Society, using adjectives that were pretty violent and stating in his own particular way how ridiculous he thought it was to portray a saint in such a fashion. The Catholic Truth Society (I must say very foolishly) sent the letter—or, at any rate, word about it—back to the rector at Stonyhurst. So the rector sent for Henry John and said, "I hear you've been writing to the Catholic Truth Society." Henry replied, "Yes, Father. I had to. Did you ever see such rubbish? Imagine making Saint Aloysius appear wearing a surplice and holding a lily! Did you ever see anything so ridiculous, Father?" The rector hadn't a chance, you see! He was defeated in the first round! He struggled along for a while and, after several rounds of defeat, he could think of nothing better to say than, "But Henry! You wrote in pencil!" And Henry stopped and said, "Oh, Father, did I? I don't know what to say, Father. I don't know what to say! Is that a mortal sin?" The boy had such great simplicity and was amazingly brilliant—a genius and at the same time a delightful boy. He had a great effect on people, and I can give you a good example.

Among the innumerable activities of the very remarkable Father Martindale was his promotion of what was called *Pax Romana,* which was an annual gathering of the young Catholic men of the time. Well, the meeting was to be held in Budapest this particular year. So Martindale wrote me and said, "I can't get enough people from the various universities to go to Budapest. Will you come and bring along two or three good boys from Stonyhurst?" I told Henry John, Christopher Devlin and Tom Burns about this invitation, and they said they very much wanted to go. Then I wrote to Father Bodkin, the Provincial, explained that I had this invitation and said I thought I'd go to Budapest. It was shortly before he was scheduled to make a visitation at Stonyhurst, and he sent me no answer before his visit. When he arrived, I met him on the staircase and he said to me, "Oh, by the way, about that going to Budapest. Rome, you know, is very difficult about these journeys now, and I'm afraid I daren't ask because you're sure to be refused." I went on to my room, and presently Henry John came along. So I said to him, "Well, Henry, I think you and the others will have to go to Budapest by yourselves, without me. I'm afraid I can't go." "Oh, can't you get permission from the Provincial?" I said, "Ssh," and he said, "Oh" and walked out of the room. About ten minutes afterward he came back to me and said,

"The Provincial wants to see you." So I went upstairs. When I came into the Provincial's room, I found him sitting there really in almost a daze. "That's an extraordinary boy. That's the most extraordinary boy I've ever met, that Henry John!" (He was still recovering from Henry's visit, you see.) Then he said, "Now, about going to Budapest. I'll tell you what. You just go. You just go." Henry was like that, you see. He was absolutely irresistible, an enchanting genius.

He had that kind of Franciscan spirituality. There was a very elegant, awfully nice man named Gilbey in Rome at the time. He now is the chaplain at Cambridge and a monsignor. You would see him at the Newmarket races or off hunting, and he was an admirable chaplain. Very elegant and very holy at the same time. Well, he and Henry John got to be great friends at the Beda, where Gilbey was studying for the priesthood. One summer they had a holiday together. Gilbey, after they had spent a lovely day, would go off to the best hotel, wherever they happened to be; but Henry would just disappear into the countryside and sleep in the crook of a tree or in a barn. He was very simple, and nature meant everything to him. Even though he had just met a person, he would be quite willing to turn over to him any money that he had, if the person appeared to need it. He was Franciscan at heart, really a child of nature.

Of those three boys who studied with me at Stonyhurst, Tom Burns is now head of the Burns and Oates publishing house in London and has done a great deal of good work for the Church. He's one of the leading Catholic laymen, I suppose, in all of England. Christopher Devlin, after a time, became a Jesuit. He wrote the life of Blessed Robert Southwell, edited Gerard Manley Hopkins' notebooks, and wrote marvelous poetry himself. An absolute top man.

Henry John was, I think, the outstanding of the three. I had very close to a father's feeling for him, an affection such as I don't think I've ever had for any other boy I've taught. I watched over him, and, when the year came to an end, he's the only boy of talent about whom I've ever said, "No, he mustn't go to Oxford. Nothing must be done to interfere with the growth of this plant. It is original; nothing must touch it. This boy must just grow and grow." Since I was going to Rome myself to study, I arranged for him to go there, too, attend classes at the Gregorian, do some theology, and other work of his own liking. I worked it out that he lived at the Beda College so that he could be completely fancy-free and develop his genius. And this indeed took place.

One could spend a lot of time speculating on what Henry John might have done, had he lived. He did enter the Jesuit Order and stayed a few years, but that didn't work out. Sometime after he left the novitiate, alas, he was drowned. He was only in his twenties then. What would have happened if he had been spared, I really don't know.

Henry's father, Augustus John, the celebrated artist, was not only a superb painter, but a great character and a lovable, gypsy giant of a man with a thunderous voice. A wholly fantastic person. He married first into a very brilliant Oxford family called the Nettleships. By that marriage he had five or six children.

Augustus John was never a Catholic, though I always felt there was a chance he might become one. He was an enormous, strong, fine person. You know, after Henry was drowned, Augustus did my portrait as a gift to me. It is supposed to be one of his best pictures and is now in Campion Hall. I must own it doesn't seem to me to be very much like me, but from the point of view of painting I suppose it is quite good. I always say to them at Campion Hall that if they go bankrupt, they'll be able to get out of it by selling that picture. I grew very fond of Augustus as the years went by.

So I did that year with these three exceptional young boys and then went off to Ireland for a short period. Now, you know the Society sends out certain men for two years to do special studies after they are ordained. These men are called biennists. They go off to Yale, Harvard, Oxford and other centers of learning. From the English Province, most go to Rome to study theology, canon law, and that sort of thing. At any rate, some of these biennists—American ones—were in Ireland when I was there and they said to me, "Oh, Father, we hear you're going to Rome." I said, "Oh, really?" And they replied, "Yes, you're going to be a professor there." It was not until later that Father Bodkin wrote to me saying, "I'm sending you to Rome." Since he didn't say anything more than that, when I was in London before leaving for Rome I went in to see him and asked just why I

Augustus John portrait

was going to Rome and what I was to do there. He was very vague in his reply; so I said, "Is it true that I'm not going to come back?" And he answered, "Well, I wouldn't be so sure of that," looking at me in his very Irish way.

When I got to Rome, Father Bea (later Cardinal Bea) was the superior in the Gesu, where I was staying. I went to him and asked him what I was to do, and he said, "Oh, you just go and consult the English Assistant. You're not doing the ordinary studies here." So I then went instead to Père Maurice de la Taille, whom I'd known and liked so much. (I am an absolute devotee of his theory of the Mass. In fact, the whole of my theology stems from de la Taille.) And he said, "Oh, you're coming on here to teach. That's what you're going to do. I've proposed you, you see." So this kind of game went on for a long time. I would go to see Father General and say, "What am I doing here?" And he'd say, "Oh, you just read and spend your time as you see fit." This went on and on until the end of the year, and then I was called up by Father Bea or the Provincial or whoever it was, and he said, "We've been desperately anxious to have an English-speaking professor at the Gregorian, and you were recommended. But we weren't certain that it would fit you and your health. After watching you this past year, we think you are obviously not very fit physically and are not the man for the job." So that ended that. I must say I had to laugh to myself, thinking of the way that they tried to keep it secret while I knew all the time. After that I did a year at Farm Street and then went on to our place at Oxford.

Campion Hall

Campion Hall

Our master at Oxford at the time was a lovely, sweet, shy, saintly man—a mathematician. But he was frightened of the world generally, and absolutely terrified of intellectual people. It was dreadful for a man like this to be at Oxford: he found himself constantly nervous and worried over it all. He didn't like the job at all, and held on solely out of duty. I'll give you an example of the sort of suffering he went through. There was a preposterously learned man at Merton College named A.E. Taylor. Later he was a professor in Edinburgh. He wrote unbelievably learned things, his books being full of the heaviest kind of knowledge. Knowing he was in Oxford at the time, I said to my master, "Oh, by the way, I see that A.E. Taylor is here in Oxford and I've invited him to dinner." He said, "Oh, oh-h-h, don't let him talk to me. He's far too learned. Oh, please keep him away from me." I said that I'd do my best, and all went well during dinner. But in the common room afterwards, the person nearest the master unfortunately got engaged talking to someone else, and I myself got to talking to yet another person, so Taylor leaned right across the room and said, "Oh, Master, I'm so anxious to ask you a question. You know, that very interesting Biblical point: there's a passage in Isaiah and also one in Jeremiah—most interesting passages they are—in connection with the signs of the zodiac, and I'm so anxious to find out what your views are on this subject." Well, that was A.E. Taylor, but it flustered the master completely.

The place we Jesuits had then was a small one leased from St. John's College in St. Giles. It was originally called Clarke's Hall; but after Father Clarke was succeeded by a certain Father O'Fallon Pope, who was an American, it became known as Pope's Hall.

Father Pope was from a very wealthy family in St. Louis. (I am told that there still are streets in St. Louis named after his family.) He was a great gentleman, extremely generous in every way. He would never allow you to do anything cheaply, but insisted you do everything grandly. An awfully considerate man, too. He'd say to you, "I understand that the light isn't very good in your room. May I just come and see about it? Would eleven o'clock tomorrow suit you for me to call in your room?" That kind of gentleman has a real charm. He had originally come to Oxford to live the life of a young gentleman at Christ Church, which was the Royal college, you see. And he lived royally, too: used to give champagne breakfasts, did a grand tour of Europe during the vacations, and all that sort of thing. Then he suddenly decided to become a priest, did his seminary studies, and eventually got into teaching theology. Later he went to the *Academia dei Nobili* in Rome, which produces so many cardinals and diplomats. It was when he finished there that he decided he'd become a Jesuit and joined the English Province. Being an Oxford man, he could come to the University and take everything on. He was absolutely unchangeable in his views and could be very obstinate. I can give you a very good example. I was sitting next to him at table one day when he shook his head and said, "You know, tea is very bad for people. Tea is very bad for people!" I said, "But, Master, I know doctors who recommend it strongly." And his reply was, "Oh, but they're not good doctors."

Even though I'm very impractical in many ways, I think I've done two big things in my life which were very practical, indeed. One was to increase enormously the finances of the English Province. Many other things that I've tried to do in my life have failed, but this one surely succeeded. When I became Provincial, the procurator for the Province—the bursar, or the treasurer, whatever you'd like to call him—a business-like man, said to me, "Oh, Father, the man who used to give me advice has left and gone off to South Africa. Do you know of anyone in the city who could advise me on investments?" I said, "Oh, I've got a friend, a great friend, a man named Robert Strauss, who is one of the top men in the city. I must introduce you to him." Well, the two of them got on like a house on fire. Robert Strauss, of course, was at the time one of the greatest financial men in the world. The result was the investments of the Province went up, even doubled. So that was one practical thing I achieved, and it was the last thing that you'd expect from me! Then, again through me, the Irish procurator (the Irish Province was rather a poor province, as you might expect) got in touch with Strauss and he doubled their investments, too.

My second accomplishment of that kind was building Campion Hall. The story involves a very distinguished architect, Sir Edwin Lutyens. He did the Whitehall Cenotaph in London, some marvelous English country houses, and then the great enormous place at Delhi, the South African War Memorial in Johannesburg, the British Embassy in Washington. Although he was not a Catholic, he was asked by Archbishop Downey to do the Catholic cathedral in Liverpool—though it never quite worked out, because the projected edifice, which was to be the great glory of Lutyens' life, would have been about the same size as St. Peter's, and the diocese began to complain that the upkeep would cost a fortune each year. The fact that he was asked, however, was extremely interesting because, some twenty years or so before, they had put out to competition the design for the Anglican cathedral in Liverpool, and the man who won it was a Catholic. (He was subsequently knighted Sir Giles Gilbert Scott.) And here the Catholic cathedral of Liverpool was to be done by Sir Edwin Lutyens, who was not a Catholic! Very curious. Well, Lutyens was regarded as the greatest living architect—indeed, the greatest architect since Sir Christopher Wren—in the British Empire. Everybody spoke of him as a great genius.

Now, in Oxford—this was back in the early 1930s—we had a house, Campion Hall, which was leased from St. John's College, right next door to it, and St. John's said that they required it back when the lease ran out. So the problem was where to go. We had an annex to Campion Hall which we owned ourselves. My predecessor was a very wonderful, sweet man, but no good at all in practical matters. So he took advice from some local priest who said to ask such-and-such an architect from Birmingham. Then this architect came along and drew up plans for the annex next door. All of us thought his plans were dreadful. Then this master was changed and I was put on as master, and I made up my mind never to have that architect's plans. The difficulty was to determine how far advanced we were towards accepting them, you see. When a person does initial plans (I've forgotten the technical terms, though I knew them then) and submits them and you do not accept them, you then pay some very small percentage of the architect's fee. But if, on the other hand, you accept the original plans and detailed plans are drawn up so that they can be acted upon and then you refuse them, you pay a much higher percentage.

Well, I understood that the previous master had never worked through the consultants and had only progressed with this architect to the stage of preliminary plans. I was determined not to have this man do my final plans. But to be sure about the matter—I think I showed myself as being rather practical here—I decided first to show the existing plans to some competent people. The director of Claridge's at the time had a boy at Stonyhurst whom I knew, and I went round to see him. He called in his brother and they examined the plans. From running a hotel they'd learned everything about what is really practical and what is not, and they said that from the point of view of practicality these plans were very bad. So then I went to somebody else who also advised me that the plans were no good at all. Well, then, I had a friend who was a rather great lady (supposedly one of the women who ran England at the time), a Lady Horner of the Jack-Horner-sat-in-a-corner family. She was a tremendously grand old lady and one of the stalwart Protestants of her time. We got on splendidly. I was the first priest she had ever allowed in her very beautiful house. So I took these plans along to her—with some cunning, I think—and said to her, "Tell me, do you think these are good plans? You know all about what is practical in running institutions." She looked at them very carefully and finally she said, "Well, Father, I'm not an authority on these things at all. Why not ask my friend Ned Lutyens?" So I said, "Well, I don't know Ned Lutyens." "Oh," she replied, "that's all right, I'll take care of that." And she went to the phone, got hold of him and said, "Ned, I've got a friend of mine here and he's got some plans on a building and he needs some advice on them. Would you see him?" He apparently agreed; so she said to me, "You can just go down there now."

I went down immediately to Lutyens' office. He looked at the plans and then brought out a beautiful album full of all the loveliest houses and buildings in England. And he said,

"Look how bad it is. Now compare that with this. Look at these windows," and so on. It was very convincing. So I said, "Well, now, will you come up to Oxford for the day and spend the night? I could get this architect—he's very probably just a provincial architect—and if he could get advice and direction from you, he'd probably be delighted because he then would be able to put up a very wonderful building and say he and Sir Edwin Lutyens had designed it." I thought that a good idea, but I didn't realize the pride of this man from Birmingham. When I proposed that to him, he wouldn't hear of it. He said simply, "Oh, my plans will do well enough as they are."

Very fortunately two or three alternative sites for our new building became available about this time, and I saw my way out of the difficulty. I asked Lutyens to come up to Oxford and took him around, first, to the old site for which the plans were drawn and, then, to the other three sites. At the third one, he said, "This is the site. This is far the best of all." So as we were walking away, I said, "Ned," (I was calling him that by this time), "that solves the great difficulty. Since I'm now going to build on new ground, I intend to start completely new plans and I can ask a different architect without hurting this other man's feelings. The question is, whom shall I ask? Do you know of any young and interesting architect whom we might get?" And he said, "Why not ask me?" So I said, "But, Ned, you have the reputation of being most appallingly expensive, and I can't possibly afford you." "Oh," he said, "I'd do it at a minimum for you. I haven't got any building in Oxford, and I should love to do it." I said, "Good!" And a great friendship developed between us after that.

Lutyens was a man of supreme genius in the line of architecture. He was the son of an Army officer, one of about fourteen children. In the old days, the Victorian days, the pensions of Army and Navy officers were very small indeed. Of the fourteen children, only three of them got what you would call a full public school education. Ned, who was one of the younger ones, used to go around to carpenters and to other artisans and found himself with this genius. He grew up in this sort of training and experience, got apprenticed to an architect, and was taken on later as an architect himself. Eventually he became a supreme architect. He remained all his life a simple and most delightful man.

Ned Lutyens made jokes, good and bad, all day long. In fact, he rarely stopped joking, and he pulled people's legs mercilessly. He was always up to his tricks, even when he was with the clergy. For instance, Archbishop Downey became devoted to him and invited him to a dinner meeting of the hierarchy. At the dinner there were toasts to the Holy Father, one to the King, and so on. Then Lutyens stood up and said, "I'd like to propose a toast. 'To the happiest nights that we've spent in our lives, the nights that we've spent with other men's wives—our mothers.' " This was always going on; you'd never know what he was going to say next. Sometimes his jokes were extraordinarily good, and other times they were very bad indeed.

I think one of the most brilliant puns I ever heard in my life was made by Ned Lutyens. He had built a chapel someplace or other and was showing a party around. One of the members of the group said to him, "Oh, Sir Edwin, we're not very good at languages. What is the meaning of the words that you've got engraved there on the face of the altar?" The words were, *Ave, Ave, Sancta.* And Lutyens replied, "That's quite simple, you know. It means two 'aves' make one 'holy.' " Now, isn't that brilliant?

This other one is a little more vulgar, but it's an awfully good pun. There was a very strong Orange north-of-Ireland group in Liverpool in those days. There used to be Catholic processions, you see, and this group would throw stones at the Catholics (and get them thrown right back, I might add!). One of the greatest nuisances was a dreadful Low Church or rationalist man who was always attacking the Catholics. I think he was a parson, I'm not sure, but his name was Longbottom. Well, he died. And immediately Lutyens drew a little grave with a tombstone and put underneath it *Vita Brevis, Ars non Longa!*

I always wanted to try and make him a Catholic. He was like a child. I think he was frightened of the dark, the step into the Church. But he used to come to Campion Hall each term for a weekend, and during benediction he'd go into a little tribune up there in the chapel he himself had designed, and you'd see him come down afterwards crying. He loved us at Campion Hall, and we loved him. He loved especially the brother who was the sacristan; he used to put his arm around him, and he was as happy as a lord there at the Hall. We grew awfully fond of him, indeed.

I remember especially his simplicity. Evelyn Waugh was at Campion Hall for dinner one night, and we went into the senior common room afterwards. Evelyn, in that abrupt way of his, turned to Lutyens and said, "Ned, isn't it about time you became a Catholic?" Lutyens began to shuffle off as usual. "Well," Evelyn Waugh continued, "you'd better hurry up, you know. Otherwise when you die, you'll begin to burn immediately." This phrase bewildered him and frightened him beyond words, because weeks after that Ned came up to me and said, "What? 'Burn immediately,' did he say, 'burn immediately'?" And I thought to myself, "That kind of phrase may do good sometimes, though I wouldn't use it myself."

Lutyens had a wife who had written a number of books. She was Lady Emily, the daughter of Lord Lytton—Bulwer Lytton. One of those women who are always seeking for spiritual satisfaction, she was forever hunting for religion, going off with Mrs. Eddy or wandering about India with some new religious leader. Another time she went to a Sacred Heart Convent to make a retreat there, to see whether she would become a sort of Catholic mystic. She was a dear woman.

When Lutyens was made president of the Royal Academy in 1938, a big luncheon was given for him and I was fortunate enough to be there. At this lunch, someone said, "Oh, Ned, congratulations on being made President of the Royal Academy. This is tremendous. You will have to make speeches now." At this Emily said, "But Ned can't make speeches." And Ned retorted, "Of course I can make speeches. I make very good speeches. Why, only a few weeks ago at an enormous banquet, I was called upon to speak; and when I got up, there was a funny old man just below the speakers' table who was very difficult to talk to. He was deaf and he kept holding a trumpet up because he wanted to hear what I was going to say. So I just poured my wine down his trumpet. I thought it a rather good start to my speech!"

He was a fantastic figure, Ned Lutyens was. One of his chance remarks comes back to me. He had criticized American buildings in those days, saying that they were built, not for the ages, but for only two years, and that then they'd be pulled down and new ones put up. Now, he was a great friend of the Architectural Association of America, so they sent him a cablegram saying how very sorry they were to hear that he'd said such a thing. His exact words in his return cable were, "Express regret, regret express." That was Lutyens.

I had a great dream for the complete Campion Hall, but we hadn't enough money. We were able to build only half of a quadrangle at the time, but Lutyens left plans for the completion of the other half, with a lot of interesting new ideas, you see. It was my hope and expectation that the other half of the quadrangle would be completed according to the Lutyens plans and ultimately turned over to the non-English

Provinces, with possibly an American minister assigned to it. Then it could be made into a kind of center for sabbatical years for the great scholars of the Society from all over the world. They could come and spend a year at Oxford and consult the Bodleian Library, and it would be something both the Society and Oxford itself could be proud of. It would be like the Institute of Advanced Studies at Princeton, you see. That was my dream, and I hoped that in time it would work out that way. It would have been glorious. But a succeeding Master of Campion Hall put on an addition, rather slap-dash and with little attention to the Lutyens plans. As a matter of fact, I believe he did it without the help of any architect at all. So that's what happened to the building.

As for the center of learning, well, the government had begun to insist that everybody should have an education diploma, even if you didn't have a degree, before you could teach in any of the schools. So for two years a man had to be trained in education, how to teach and all the rest, you see. There are always a number of men in the Society, especially in the English Province, who are not much from the point of view of learning but who can teach quite well even though they haven't got degrees. So I set up a place for practically all religious orders to seek the necessary diplomas. But my successor Provincial came on and he closed it down. (Incidentally, the English cardinals and the bishops were furious at this.) Now, most of these people couldn't possibly qualify for degrees at Oxford, but it is true that just by studying education they could get diplomas. And this is what happened: the new Provincial opened up Campion Hall to them and let them get diplomas from Oxford. So I saw all my dreams of a center of learning go for naught, and the whole quality of the place and the men—the elite—disappeared. I don't think now there's any chance at all for what I once had hoped would have happened. That depressed me dreadfully at the time.

Then, in 1945, I became Provincial of the English Province. In certain ways I enjoyed the assignment, but it did involve awful and agonizing problems. As you can imagine, sometimes a person is in great difficulties, and situations arise that would break one's heart. On the other hand, there was the chance to have so may projects started, to test one's ideas, to make so many changes, to really do things. And there were so many nice persons one dealt with.

Modernism

It is astonishing to me to see the changes in attitudes and atmosphere within the Church on so many things since my
days as a young man. I came in just at the very end of the
modernist movement, free of it, but knowing all of its
tragedies. It was a very grim moment in the history of the
Church, and no wonder. Pius X thought that modernism
was a most dangerous "summing up of all heresies," as he
put it. I used to go about and find all sorts of persons infected by it, and they were nearly always among the most
brilliant minds of the time. For instance, I can recall a convert clergyman at the Assumption Convent in London. He
had gone completely modernist, and they were letting him
live out his life there at the convent. He had a most miserable
existence. Man after man was infected by it and fell by the
way.

As you know, the essence of modernism, almost exclu-
sively confined to theological or spiritual circles within the
Church, corresponded in a certain manner with one of the
dangerous views going on outside the Church. Pragmatism,
you will remember, was the rage around 1900. William
James and the rest in many parts of the world said: "The

truth is simply that which works. There is no such thing as a static or conceptual truth. It is just what works." Modernism roughly came to this, saying: "It doesn't make much difference about the fact of Christ's rising from the dead, or whether Christ actually died for man on the Cross; but the value lies in the fact of the testimony coming down to us as liberating the soul, as providing a rich experience for man. That is what counts. The mere fact or concept of it is always out of date; the concept has to be framed in language which is of very little use, except possibly for one period, and therefore all these scholastic and other philosophical thoughts are no good. But there is this *enormous* value which attached to the Christian liberation and redemption and union." That view came into popularity and took possession of many of the most interesting minds of the Church. Then it was ruthlessly destroyed by Pius X. If the destruction hadn't been ruthless, the heresy probably would have gone on.

To me it is very odd that the movement is as dead as a dodo now. The next generation had no interest in it, and I came on just at the end of it, knowing all about it, seeing all these elder men besieged by it. Then as I passed middle age, I forgot it myself because the people I talked to were not interested. (There is now a certain new phase of it—different, but interesting and slightly dangerous.) But there for one moment it had looked as if the whole Church was tottering, as if there was no way any longer of holding on to the conceptual truths, the dogmatic truths. Yet the extirpation brought desperately sad losses: in France, for instance, the great Loisy; in England, Tyrrell. Lots of others were touched by it. Some left the Church and later came back again. Interesting people like Algar Thorold, who was infected by it for a few years. (He was the son of the Bishop of Winchester and is the uncle of the present Count de la Bédoyère, who writes so many books and edits *The Catholic Herald* and visits in the United States.) In Italy there were a large number of people who fell: Buonaiuti and all sorts of interesting people, terribly sad tragedies. Pius X crushed it and crushed it remorselessly. He was a saint, but he was hated—actually hated—by the modernists. Von Hügel used to say, "That peasant Pope, he doesn't understand." They couldn't bear him. They used to attribute the opposition partly to him and partly to Cardinal Merry del Val, the Papal Secretary of State, saying, "That Spaniard never understands anything intellectual." Merry del Val was actually a sweet and lovely man, a very handsome and strong man, with great Spanish integrity. But I can still remember a young Australian priest in Rome telling me that he used to get up each morning and look anxiously in *L'Osservatore Romano* to see if his name was down as suspended or excommunicated!

The Abbé Duchesne story is a very amusing one. He escaped condemnation, but he hated the whole thing, too. All the intellectuals did. Somebody went to Abbé Duchesne's room, in Rome, found him packing, and asked, "Are you leaving?" He said, "Yes, I'm just going off to Egypt." "For how long?" "Until the death of Herod." Well, that was the attitude of the time, showing an extraordinary violence of opinion.

A good many Jesuits felt the effects. I was told, for example, that the ordination of my beloved Father Woodlock was delayed because he spoke to a person who was under strong suspicion of being a modernist. The ordinations of all sorts of people were delayed. Nobody's books could be published. The whole thing put the clock back enormously at the time.

I have no personal knowledge of Father George Tyrrell, but I knew all about him from many of his friends who had known and loved him greatly. He was that kind of Protestant saturnine Irish, the Dean Swift type—one type of Irishman who is so far from being what they caricatured him as in England: the roistering type. Rather, he had a cold, hard mind. He was taken off by Shaw a little bit in *John Bull's Other Island* as the real Irishman: he may be emotional, but his mind is strong, and he is a bitter, cynical man. Tyrrell was that type. He was of a Protestant Irish family. He had a cousin who afterwards became a Catholic and later became a peer and was at one time the top English diplomat in Egypt. A distant relation of his was the famous don at Balliol, F.F. Urquhart, probably the most fantastic Catholic of his time. Then there was a Professor Tyrrell, the great classical scholar who edited volume after volume of Cicero's letters— one of the great characters of Trinity College, Dublin.

Tyrrell was an outstandingly brilliant man, but quite ugly, with a broad forehead and a face that tapered down to almost no chin under a large mouth. I remember hearing a very wicked story of one seminarian going up to another, the famous Father Leslie Walker, and saying, "I congratulate you." Walker replied, "Why? Have I got my degree?" And the first seminarian said, "No, but Tyrrell's left the Society, and you're the ugliest man in it now." Well, that's the kind of reputation he had from the point of view of looks.

But apparently he could be very attractive in personal conversation and could win people to him. He made tremendous disciples who were absolutely devoted to him. He was a man of prayer and used to spend hours and hours praying. He was a most wonderful writer, extraordinarily brilliant; in fact, his writing was very likely the best of his time. But I think the secret to his character, and to his unhappy life, was that he always like to sing outside choruses. He could never belong to a group. He was that kind of lonely fighter who, if people held a certain viewpoint, was himself bound to hold the opposite. (That is a trait, again, which I think is characteristic of certain Irishmen.) He loved and was loved by a group of distinguished Jesuits when he joined the Society. Father Herbert Thurston was an early friend of his; Father Daniel Considine, Father Hungerford-Pollen, Father John Gerard, Father Joseph Rickaby and others around about that time were his contemporaries. I am told, and am prepared to believe, that he was by far the ablest of them all. This may surprise some partisans of Thurston, but Thurston wasn't what I call a thinker. Rather, he was a scholar. The essays which Tyrrell wrote were original, creative thinking, and everybody recognized this though they might not have agreed with what the man had to say. Incidentally, Thurston and Tyrrell were great friends, and Thurston stuck to him almost to the end. You see, Tyrrell was such an attractive person, and Thurston had all the finest qualities of his time and was a man of tremendous integrity and fierce loyalty, and Tyrrell was his friend. It was only when it came out that Tyrrell, even when he was a Jesuit, had been writing under an assumed name attacks upon the Society and upon the Church—expressing the modernist views—then Thurston found it awfully hard to forgive him this wrong. That he should live one life and profess being one thing and at the same time write under an assumed name against all this, such duplicity upset Thurston very much. As I say, Tyrrell had to sing outside choruses. At least this is my theory.

When he was in his theology, the theologate was a house of ours in North Wales called St. Bueno's. There was on the faculty a funny old German professor of theology called Father Tepe, a rather out-of-date theologian. Now, some brilliant French Jesuits who had just been driven out of France had taken up residence in a prison about twenty or thirty miles away, where they were temporarily continuing their house of theology. They had there some exceptionally able men, among them a famous theologian who wrote a tremendous article in the *Dictionnaire de Théologie,* and all sorts of other great men. Well, Tyrrell slipped over there, you see, got the theses of these French Jesuits, came back to St. Bueno's and passed them all around the class to be used against Tepe. As you can imagine, this caused considerable trouble.

Later Tyrrell was appointed professor in philosophy at St. Mary's Hall. When he arrived there, he found the faculty was all Suarezian; so he brought St. Thomas down into the classroom, and they had to read the text of St. Thomas. He was a tremendous Thomist for a while. Then he wrote some brilliant articles which led to his meeting Baron von Hügel, the great European scholar with a universal reputation. The Baron was quite surprised when he found Tyrrell didn't know German and had never heard of certain names in the theological and philosophical world. He told the young Jesuit, "You are not up-to-date. You do not know the scholars." Tyrrell was swept off his feet for a time, although he ultimately came to despise von Hügel. Despite the fact that he was an able man himself—abler, really, than von Hügel—he was nevertheless carried away and began to think that Thomism and all scholasticism was dreadfully provincial. Then he became involved with modernism and the rest. And that went on for some time. Oh, such troubles followed! Yet he was much loved and many people stood by him.

Well, Tyrrell then started being taken around to the Souls, which was a Society where the greatest minds in England and Europe met, the ablest scientists and theologians and philosophers of the day, and he could more than hold his own amongst them. He was so brilliant. Then, more and more, his writings fell under suspicion, and he be-

gan to show himself bitter towards the Order. Finally he left
the Society. There was awful trouble with the Spanish General of the time, Father Martin. The General was very kind to
him, but Tyrrell wrote terrible things against him. He finally
ended up with only one real confidante, a tremendous disciple of his, a woman called Maude Petre. She belonged to a
very old family, the Lords Petre. Tyrrell was supposed to
have said that she had only the brain of a squirrel; but she
wrote several books, and her letters show her to have been a
very intelligent woman. After his death she wrote a biography of him.

At around the age of fifty he got this Bright's disease,
which began to affect his brain. In any case, he then began
rapidly to go down, and he said to Maude Petre, "Don't let
me die like a dog, will you?" He was terribly ill, and she
sent for the Franciscans from Storrington not far away; and
word was, I suppose, telegraphed to Farm Street. Father
Thurston couldn't be reached, but Father Hungerford-Pollen
came down. When the fathers arrived, they found he was
too far gone to be sure that he could even make response
with his hand. And in this way he died. Bishop Amigo, who
was up from Gibraltar, was a very obstinate man and he may
have had directions from Rome, I don't know, but at any
rate he refused Tyrrell a Catholic burial. So there was this
meeting of Tyrrell's friends. Abbé Henri Bremond, who had
also been a Jesuit, was there. (There were three Bremonds,
you know. I think all three were Jesuits, but two of them left
the Society. One of them remained and became a great Pla-

tonist, taught in Jersey and was much loved. Father Norris Clark studied under him, and so did Father William Erdozain. I think he taught at Fordham for a while.) But the Bremond who was Tyrrell's friend was a very strange man. He became an Academician before he died. He was quite brilliant, but I should have thought he was a lightweight intellectually. He was a good *litterateur* and when he got outside of the Society, he wrote, "The net is broken and we are free." So he came to the funeral even though Bishop Amigo had refused a Catholic burial. Many of Tyrrell's friends turned up there, von Hügel and the rest. Bremond came over from France and gave an address, a panegyric at the grave. He was immediately suspended by Amigo, but it didn't make any difference to him: he could just go back to France, outside Amigo's diocese. And that was the end of poor Tyrrell.

There are those who feel rather strongly against von Hügel and Miss Petre. They were at Tyrrell's deathbed, and the Franciscan priest is said to have asked them, as his closest friends (Tyrrell was unconscious then), what his probable dispositions were. Von Hügel was supposed to have replied that Tyrrell would most probably wish the last sacraments and reconciliation with Rome, but not at the price of a complete recantation. Therefore the Franciscan gave conditional absolution, but then Tyrrell recovered consciousness just for a while and conversed for a very brief period with the priest, who then gave absolution *in extremis*. Tyrrell did not recover consciousness again but received extreme unction, and it looked as though possibly he had been reconciled with the Church. Then Miss Petre wrote a letter to *The London Times* in which von Hügel concurred, setting out the Baron's earlier remarks to the effect that Tyrrell would not have wanted reconciliation at the price of a complete recantation. There is some evidence that this is the point where Bishop Amigo stepped in. As I say, there are those who are offended that von Hügel went through his whole life never being condemned, and yet was the one who seemingly threw Tyrrell, a known reckless man, into the fray.

But that's not quite the situation, it seems to me. I think that, if you put yourself back into that time, you will find his enemies accused von Hügel of being a leader of modernism and yet escaping condemnation by Rome. There was a lot of criticism that way, but I think it was unjustified. I think the general verdict since has been that it was unjustified. The Baron was a very firm Catholic in his own strange fashion— a very strange fashion, I admit—but a most saintly and holy man. Everybody adored him and thought him one of the most spiritual of men—much more so, I would think, than people now regard Albert Schweitzer. He was in a way the greatest figure in the spiritual world at that time, but he had desperately strong convictions, you see. He felt it would be an outrage if an attempt or pretension were made at the last moment that Tyrrell didn't really hold those views which he and they all held, and which they felt Tyrrell had strongly held. They regarded it as one of those matters which make a great difference. (Only recently, there was trouble over Gilbert Murray's death—the deathbed conversion controversy.) They felt the priests might have taken hold of Tyrrell when he wasn't fully *compos*—a man who stood for all these things which they had stood with him on, and had been hurt and wounded for—and they sincerely believed this would be enormously to the benefit of the Church to get hold of. They felt it was only the recalcitrants, the backward men, the "peasant Pope," who were trying to stop the movement. They thought that the great hope of the Church was to take hold of these views, you see, and they were not going to yield. Actually, that was their point, and, from their view, a very strong one. As for depriving poor Tyrrell of a Christian burial, they did feel that he had behaved that way, had given up not only the Catholic Church but Anglicanism as well, and had shown no sign of any going back at all. He was a tiger-like fighter before he fell ill. Therefore they felt that this man who was one of their great protagonists should not be turned into a namby-pamby at the last moment. I must say I see their point myself.

It is hard to say just what there was about modernism that so vitally attracted Tyrrell. Probably he was influenced by the out-of-dateness of the attitude and teaching of the Church at the time. You don't realize, I think, how much the philosophers and theologians of the Church have come on since then. My goodness, look at what poor Newman had to go through! If we only knew what real temptations that great person probably suffered when he went to Rome and found such third-rate men! There was only one man—Peroni, a Jesuit—who seemed to Newman to be first-rate. It was a very bad period for the Church. Owing to the French Revolution and liberal governments, and lots of very weak people in the papacy, and the fall of the Jesuits, everything had collapsed all over the place. That's why there was this enormous movement in France, which was premature. Lammenais and Lacordaire sought a liberal Catholicism which didn't rely upon reason but on a curious thing called faith, a special tradition of faith. Fortunately the Church in its unerring way saw this wouldn't do. It said that that was too early a summer, too early a spring, and they cracked down on it, even though they didn't properly understand what it was all about.

Speaking of Lammenais, I once wrote a piece for *Reader's Digest,* which was never published, saying how I think God has, in His love, endowed all people in their last moments with enormous grace; but in the case of those who have publicly denied Him, God doesn't allow it to be shown what He does in their last moments. And I cited Tyrrell and Lammenais, who went through the same tortures when Rome wouldn't have them. He was a very excitable, nervous person. (Incidentally, he had a brother who founded two religious orders and was a saint.) I remember reading a life of Lammenais in which there was a record of how he was kept away from any Catholic getting near him when he was dying. But a Catholic woman did penetrate the guard and spoke to him, and he paid no attention to her. So she turned away. As she got to the door, she looked back just as he turned his head, and she saw a tear trickle down his face. He was dead in a few days. And it looks as though it is, well, the policy of God in the case of a public sinner, to say, "You can't do this and get away with it as far as the world is concerned." Tyrrell, I think, had to endure a great deal in that way. Please God he is in heaven!

Tyrrell felt desperately the third-rateness of things in the Church. And much of it was pretty third-rate. He felt that men like Father Joseph Rickaby were terrible lightweights. I myself realized years afterward, when I got to know my beloved Joe Rickaby and others who had such reputations, that if you really examined them, you found that they were quite children in terms of depth of thinking and in the sense of power to grasp situations. I think there has been a tremendous change since then among the Jesuits and especially among the Dominicans. This is particularly apparent in France, where there developed this marvelous set of men, of whom Teilhard de Chardin was the last. He was just coming up in that period, as was Rousselot, who was probably the greatest intellect of the modern generation. The latter was killed in the First World War when he was just a young priest, but he was there in 1914, ten years after Tyrrell. These men set a pattern of thinking which just left behind all that was going on when Tyrrell came on the scene.

I am told that Tyrrell in one of his books—I think it was *Faith of the Millions*—had a review of a book about Lammenais by a man named Gibson. This was written about ten years before Tyrrell had his own trouble, and there is apparently a painful parallel between Lammenais and Tyrrell in Tyrrell's analysis at that time of the Lammenais situation. Even the adjectives used to describe the man were adjectives later used to describe Tyrrell himself. And Tyrrell spoke of Lammenais' imaginary dilemma between freedom of thought and ecclesiastical authority—which ultimately was the shoal on which he himself foundered! It is extraordinarily interesting, isn't it?

Of course, Tyrrell did meet many intellectual people, compared with the average priest trained just in scholastic thought. When he moved out amongst all the people whom von Hügel introduced him to—the infinite variety and brilliance of minds—I can understand the man thinking, "Good gracious me, I've lived in a completely provincial society!" And, as I say, he liked singing against the chorus always, so he turned around and said: "What rubbish all this scholasticism is compared with what these people have done! I must improve it." I think he believed this really quite strongly, and I think his wonderful writings showed that he had an enormous amount to say.

You see, compared with what's allowed now, with what's going on now in various theological houses, Tyrrell was in many ways rather conservative—for example, as far as the scriptures are concerned. There is today a liberality of treatment of the New Testament which I myself find, I must own, quite shocking. Well, when Tyrrell was writing, you couldn't really say that the rib of Adam wasn't a real rib, or that the serpent wasn't a real devil, without falling under disciplinary action. You can see what that kind of thing did to a man of Tyrrell's ability. Of course, in the end he sadly mixed up what he wanted with what was essential. But the power of his words! He had a controversy with a wonderful French Jesuit, a man who wrote a book on the Trinity. This man said, "I stand by the Creed," and Tyrrell challenged him. Well, you should see how Tyrrell attacked! Like a fierce dog, tearing at things— a real Irishman of the acute mind. On and on he went in savage irony. There you saw his bitterness. Wrong so many times, but still a mind so able. I'd like very much to have crossed swords with him.

While George Tyrrell was known for his kindness to young people, one story which I know and which is connected with a Father Cornelius Clifford is not to Tyrrell's credit, I think. Cornelius Clifford was an American boy, an extremely good-looking, lovely boy, a kind of *enfant terrible* in the days before the American Jesuits had reached their high stature of intellect. They really felt he was too much for them, so they sent him over to Belgium, and from there he joined the English Province. He joined it at a time when it was full of these relatively able men—interesting men, at any rate. From the point of view of pure intellectual power, Tyrrell was outstanding; Thurston was there as an extraordinarily able historian and critic and scholar; Father Daniel Considine was a very saintly man; Hungerford-Pollen was a convert of the Newman generation. That's not all of them, but they made a very interesting group. Cornelius Clifford joined this crowd and was as happy as the day was long, because he met men of his own mettle. He took especially to Tyrrell (I gathered this from Clifford himself), who recognized his ability, made a disciple of him and used him as a kind of stalking horse to put out his own views. The result was that poor Cornelius Clifford ran into great trouble and finally, I think, was dismissed from the Society and came back to the United States, where the bishops wouldn't so much as look at him. Ultimately he got a small church in New Jersey, and there he lived and labored and accumulated several thousand books which he bequeathed to Father Gregory Balkstead, then the headmaster of Portsmouth Priory, a private school.

Well, there was a group of laymen (it seems to me that laymen save the Church) in New York: Coudert, the remarkable Alexis Carrell, Tom Woodlock and several others—a closely-knit group and very fond of one another. They recognized this genius hidden away out there in this New Jersey village; and, while they didn't take him away from his village, they did secure for him a membership in the Century Club in New York and got him a kind of professorship in medieval theology at Columbia University.

When I came over to the States in 1935 on my first visit and was with my dear friend, Msgr. McMahon, who should appear but this beautiful, rubicund old man with white hair, Father Cornelius Clifford! He immediately threw his arms about me because I was from the English Province, you see, and all the memories of Daniel Considine, George Tyrrell and all the rest had risen in his mind. I felt so warm to him that when I went back to England I remembered, along a much greater line, how St. Thomas Aquinas, when one of his beloved Dominicans had died, asked that an annual feast be held in honor of his deceased brother. So I went to Tom Woodlock and asked him to have a portrait of Father Clifford painted by some American artist and to collect a little money, just enough to support a feast every year in his honor. The portrait was done by a man named Peck or Pack. At any rate, there is now at Campion Hall a painting of Father Cornelius Clifford, and every year there is the Cornelius Clifford dinner. So we remember him that way. Some of his friends sent him over to England before he died at the age of seventy-seven, and he went round then and had a glorious time and was so happy all over again. His was an extraordinary story. Unfortunately, he never wrote anything that I know of, though he was a very brilliant man.

Thus far I have spoken a good deal about Tyrrell, whom I didn't know, but have said almost nothing about von Hügel, whom I did know and who is by and large much better known. This is probably because Tyrrell interests me more. While the Baron was truly a remarkable man, I myself don't think his mind compared with Tyrrell's. He was rather more like Lord Acton: a sort of international scholar, knowing what everyone else has said, composing as it were anthologies, doing lovely works on all views held by various other persons.

I met him in his old age. I was then a very young man and admired him greatly. He seemed to become rather fond of me, too. While I did not see him too frequently, we did have many interesting talks and we corresponded to a certain extent. I think I still have some of his letters.

His father had been Austrian ambassador at Milan, but he himself was educated largely by private tutors, abroad and in England, and was not a university man. Yet, by prodigious reading and much contact with great minds, he became very learned. I remember his saying to me that the two greatest figures he had ever met were Abbé Huvelin and Cardinal Newman. It is a very complicated matter to portray him accurately, much more so to evaluate him. He was a very good Catholic indeed—a holy and spiritual man, a saintly figure. For anyone to dare say a word against him or criticize him would cause his friends to lash out at one with murder in their eyes. But he *was* a curious mixture of a man and, indeed, a bit *odd*. He was a man of very poor judgment about others—for example, his own daughter: he tried to teach her so much that she went cracky. He was a real German type, speaking English with a heavy guttural accent. I would not be inclined to say that he really had much of a sense of humor. On the other hand, he could be very mischievous.

I can remember one instance where he told a story about Newman which caused some of the Cardinal's friends considerable distress: how one of the Newman converts—Dalgairns, an exceptional man—joined the Oratorian Community at Birmingham, where Newman was in residence at the time. Something happened which caused a rift between the two, and the Cardinal, always a high-strung person, was so upset by the break that he could not bring himself even to speak to Dalgairns. The latter bore it for about a week and then suddenly burst into the room where Newman was sitting and said, "Father, Father, speak to me! I cannot bear it—not having you talk to me." And Newman, overwrought, seemed unable to speak. At which Dalgairns said, "Father, if you won't speak to me, I cannot bear to live in this house and will have to leave." But Newman, his hands grasping at the arms of the chair, writhed but seemed totally unable to get a word out; so Dalgairns rushed from the room and went straight off to Father Faber in London, where the other Oratory house was located. This story was quite distressing to friends of Newman like the Wards and others, as von Hügel must have known it would be.

I once referred to von Hügel as "a Triton among minnows" in an article I wrote. By that I meant that he was so outstanding, his stature so far above most of the Catholics of his time. He was not a priest, he did not have the priestly responsibilities, and as a matter of practice did not seek the *imprimatur* on his writings. Of this practice he once said to me, "If I wrote under an *imprimatur,* I'd be under the burden of the responsibility of the whole Church." As a matter of fact, he wrote in such a very heavy style and his writings were for the most part so difficult to read and understand that Rome never bothered with him. When he wrote *The Mysti-*

cal Element, volumes on St. Catherine of Genoa, he himself said he expected only six or eight persons to read them; and for a long time it was in fact little read, though it has now come to be regarded as something of a great book, despite the fact that much of what it says is as dead as a dodo. To my mind you get the whole of von Hügel there. An intensely spiritual man, he was benumbed, exalted, by scholarship; and, knowing everybody in the world of scholars worth knowing at that time, he became interested in learning everything that had been said or written on a subject and what he regarded as the "last word" in critical scholarship. That part of what he had to say is pretty dead, it seems to me, because what he appeared to mean by the "last word" was not the *ultimate,* but merely the latest or most modern. He also wrote articles for encyclopedias— the *Encyclopedia Britannica,* I believe. When he was off on his scholarship theory, examination of texts and the like, he wasted a good deal of time; but when he wrote his own stuff, he made some genuine contributions. He had a wonderful spiritual insight, and a good deal of what he said in *The Mystical Element* has passed into all spiritual literature.

I suppose that in his day he was one of the great spiritual and intellectual forces of the world. He was the Schweitzer of his time and, indeed, much more than that. I once did a talk on him over the BBC. (I may even have the manuscript in my room at Farm Street.) It was a labor of love. I had been very much attracted to the Baron and he stimulated me greatly, as he did everyone he met.

Let me tell you a story to illustrate his amazing effect on people. About 1917, during the War, I was back at Oxford for a while and Father Plater, the then Master of Campion Hall, had von Hügel in for lunch. At table there were Father Plater, Father Martindale, von Hügel, myself and, strangely enough, a very simple, uneducated Australian Tommy, a bushman type whom Father Plater had befriended and had into Campion Hall now and then just to give him a square meal and have a friendly talk. Well, early on in the course of lunch the discussion got off onto some abstruse topic on which the Baron talked for most of the meal, his face lit up, making many gestures, and warming to his subject while his food got increasingly cold. When we got up from table, Martindale turned to this Australian and said, "I'm awfully sorry. We got off on this subject that could not have been of any possible interest to you, and you must have been bored beyond words." To which the bushman replied in his squeaky voice, "I didn't understand a word of it, not one word, but I could sit and listen to that man for a week!" Now, there's a real compliment: this remarkable genius captivating a listener just by the way he spoke and gestured. There was something about him that just carried you away.

I can still remember another time when he was at Oxford. He had just delivered a lecture, and I asked him how it had gone. "Ah!" he said, "I did my best. But I thank God for my deafness because during the discussion period I think they were rather critical of me, but I couldn't hear and was able to say my prayers." There's something very lovely about that.

Again, just after von Hügel died, I was fortunate enough to become a member of the London Society for the Study of Religion. There were some splendid minds in this group of men and they were very serious about the discussions at their meetings. But if, in the course of the discussions, someone quoted the late von Hügel, the others would say in respectful awe: "Oh! The Baron said that? Oh! Did he say that?" And whatever the Baron had said, Unitarian, Jew, Catholic and the rest would all accept without more, so strong was the impact of this spiritual genius of the first water. Wherever he went, he seemed to produce that effect. But, naturally, that dies with the man and those who have known him personally.

I have been thinking recently of something von Hügel once said to me. "Do not forget. There is always a twenty-year lag between the ideas which originate with the intelligentsia and then go down and down until you hear them spread among the people. It takes, as I say, twenty years before these ideas work themselves out into action on the part of the people." And that seems to be profoundly true.

The Baron said another interesting thing to me which I still remember. He said, "Notice, when the French Revolution began, the aristocracy on the whole were supposed to be Catholics, but they were rotten at the core. The intelligentsia—that is, the lawyers, the professors, the university crowd and the rest—were growing rotten and were becoming agnostics and atheists. But the people were still soundly Catholic. Yet in 1900, after a hundred years, what has happened? It has gone full circle. The aristocracy have become good practicing Catholics, the intelligentsia are returning to the Church, but the people have lost their faith. The Church has lost the people." I found that very interesting and, as I say, I've never forgotten it. So you see, we can't afford to let the universities have all their own way.

I think the Society of Jesus has done very good work in its time, but I believe that today it is, in a sense, a burnt-out power. I have said this for a long time now; I have kept on warning my beloved Jesuit friends, saying, "Your day is over." Twenty years ago when I first said that, they looked at me with absolute contempt. Now that the liturgical movement is sweeping in, the Benedictines are coming into their own, and wherever they move, they succeed. And all the lay people are carrying missals and taking part in the Mass and leaving the Jesuits to their little devotions. It happened in German, it happened in France, and it has happened in a mild way in England.

The Jesuits' great power in the past has been their emancipation from stereotyped thinking. Whenever anything good came along, the Jesuits up until now have always been among the leaders in adopting it. For instance, the revival of Thomism: though the Society was supposed to be irrevocably committed to its own Jesuit philosophers, the leaders in the Thomist movement were Jesuits. Again in mystical prayer, you'll find one after another of the Jesuits in the forefront. In scripture studies, again the Jesuits were leading. And similarly in many other movements. That's been one of the great strengths of the Society, I think, showing its enormous vitality, its capacity for change, being able to learn and move from established positions and take on new things. Naturally, there's always been a group within the Society who tend to become stereotyped and say, "Oh, I don't approve of that sort of thing. It is not what I am accustomed to. Let's have more *bona mors*." But everywhere in life you always have a tussle in accomplishing change.

So you can see why I fight for my beloved Jesuits. Still, I do think that, in a way, their life is threatened now. Let me give you an illustration of what I mean. The famous Abbot Butler, the man who wrote the books on western mysticism and on the First Vatican Council, used to narrate how, being in London, he called in at our Farm Street Church and heard this message being read out: "Today is Palm Sunday. There will be *Bona Mors* at four o'clock this afternoon." That summed it up, you see. Nothing about the beautiful meaning of Palm Sunday, beyond its being an occasion for a long-established devotion on behalf of the faithful departed!

Again, on the Feast of Candlemas—one of the loveliest feasts of the year, when everyone ought to be carrying candles—my American Jesuit friends do not seem to pay much attention to it. But the next day is the Feast of St. Blaise, and there's a superstition about putting two candles under your throat, so the whole community is crowding into the chapel!

Early Jesuit Friends

What I could say about my English Jesuit friends doesn't seem to me to be of very great interest. The biographies of two or three of them have been published, and I really haven't got anything much to add. However, I am so constantly reminded of one or another of them that I would like to say just a few words about them.

When I was young I knew Father Bernard Vaughan rather well. He was one of the most tremendous figures of his time. How great a personage he was one cannot really appreciate today. Wherever he went, people used to recognize him on sight. Whether he went to China or Japan or the United States or wherever in the world, they'd always heard of Father Vaughan. For example, when he came to America, some tribe of Indians made him a chief. He was one of the three or four most popular figures in the world at the time. I remember someone telling me that in the early days of movies, when they'd have a "News of the Week," they'd show pictures of a person like Lloyd George and there'd be considerable clapping, but then they'd put on Bernard Vaughan and there'd be far more applause. He became one of those persons who sparked popular interest. I couldn't possibly say exactly what there was about him that did it. He was a marvelous talker. In fact, he was the only man I've ever known whose gift of telling stories was such that, after he had told good stories for an hour or an hour and a half, you still wanted him to go on. Now, you know when the average person tells stories, even when a Bob Hope cracks jokes, after a time you feel like saying, "Oh, stop it. We've had enough. We've enjoyed you enormously, but now you're getting tiresome." But Bernard Vaughan was such a spellbinder that he could go on telling his stories and you'd long for him to continue; and when he would suggest that he had to be running along, people would say, "Oh, no, don't. Please don't stop. Tell us some more."

He belonged, you know, to a very great family. It is little realized that in his immediate family, I think all but one of ten or eleven children became priests or nuns. One of his brothers became a cardinal, the Cardinal Vaughan who succeeded Cardinal Manning. Another one became an archbishop in Australia. (Whether that was the same man who also became abbot up in Scotland, I'm not sure.) Then there was Father Kenelm Vaughan, an astonishing man and practically a saint, who started a religious order. There was our Father Bernard Vaughan; and then there was another Bishop Vaughan, an auxiliary bishop up north. The one brother who didn't become a religious was a colonel in the army and the family goes on through him. Yes, they were a wonderful family, the Vaughans of Courtfield. (You may recall my speaking of a fantastic man named Frederick Rolfe, Baron

Corvo. Well, in his book *Hadrian the Seventh* he speaks of a Cardinal Courtley, and that was Vaughan of Courtfield, you see.)

So Bernard Vaughan was one of the youngest of that group. He was at Stonyhurst as a boy, and even there he showed this amazing gift of speaking and joking and telling brilliant stories. He never was a scholar or anything of that sort, but he simply captured the imagination of the whole of the world. Somebody once told me about his taking a little voyage from Liverpool, where he happened to be staying, to the Isle of Man, between Ireland and England. I suppose he'd been doing a great deal of preaching, and the rector suggested he go and have a holiday on the Isle of Man. Somehow it got known on board the boat that Father Bernard Vaughan was among the passengers, and all those lovely simple people from Lancaster and Yorkshire, mill girls and all the rest, sought him out and greeted him, saying, "Ay, Father Vaughan! Ay, Father Bernard Vaughan! Wonderful, wonderful! Just want to shake your hand, Father." And there he stood on deck, like an emperor surrounded by his court, you see.

He was a truly fantastic person. And he had a beautiful character. They say he went to confession every day of his life—not that I think that's necessarily a merit, but it shows at any rate that he was a very fervent man. He was extremely good to all young people. He ran a club in the East End of London which produced a wonderful effect and impression on the people of that area. Altogether, he was an adorable person. He had an extraordinary, fascinating personality which caught hold of people, and those who tried to imitate him were complete failures. Speaking of him stirs up great memories.

Also of Bernard Vaughan's generation, and the man I loved most of all the Jesuits of my own Province, was Father Charles Plater. I was at Oxford with Father Plater and knew him well. He came from what was originally a Polish family. He was a rather brilliant boy at Stonyhurst and was taken up by the great Jesuit of that time, Father John Gerard. Then he entered the Society. He was always regarded as such a gay person, witty and laughing, and so winning that he could make you do just about anything he wanted you to do.

By the time he had finished his scholasticate, he was already a name known throughout England because he had started the Retreat Movement. He also started the Catholic Social Guild. Those were two tremendous movements, you see. This was all before he became a priest, and you'd have thought that he would have been pushed on to something truly big when he was ordained. But the Provincials in England never seemed to know their men very well and tended to say, "Oh, there's a gap there; let's just fill it with someone." Father Plater knew some Latin, and there was such a desperate need for men that they put him down for teaching Latin. When he finished theology, they happened to need a professor of psychology in the house of studies; so poor Plater, the man who had started the Retreat Movement and was one of the greatest known Catholic figures in England, was sent off to teach psychology, a subject which he had never really studied, though he had done his course in the subject. But he did this stint with gaiety, though he obviously wasn't particularly good in the field. Next, when there was a gap in a high school for a teacher of Latin and Greek in the top grade, he was sent off to teach Latin and Greek there. Then one day he came down to recreation and said, "You know, there's a new Master of Campion Hall. Guess who it is!" So all sorts of guesses were made, and when they were finished he said, "Well, you're all wrong. I'm the new Master of Campion Hall!" And he met with a complete guffaw of laughter because no one would believe it!

When he came on to Oxford he was so wonderful, really. He did everything right. Everybody loved him. It was during the First World War, and there was a hospital near Oxford. Every wounded soldier got to know Father Plater's name. He was a simple kind of person, so loving and so unselfish, and they adored him. I myself thought he was one of the loveliest men I ever met. He was a tremendous worker. Even though he was dog-tired, he'd go on for almost twenty-four hours without stopping. You'd see him taking snuff there in his chair and dozing off, and then suddenly somebody would mention that there was a sick man out in the hospital twenty miles away. His face would instantly light up, he'd get in his old battered car, and off he'd go to the hospital.

I remember being told that the Mayor of Blackpool asked Father Plater to come and deliver a big address there. Father was utterly exhausted from other work when he arrived, but he gave his talk, and then the Mayor insisted upon giving him a lunch. A friend of mine who was there said you could see him trying to keep himself awake. Then they dragged him off to some big entertainment—a variety show, I think. And there he was, completely tired out, when someone said to him, "You know, there's a hospital just outside Blackpool (this was still in 1917 or 1918, I suppose) where the wounded Tommies are." "What? I'll have to drop over there." Just like that, he excused himself and went out to the hospital. There he played on the piano and banjo and the rest, and put them all to bed about ten or eleven o'clock at night. Then he came back to Oxford, refreshed at last, full of life and rejoicing. He was a wonderful man, to my mind, and his influence on me was very great. I was more drawn to him than to anybody else I have known.

When I left Oxford and went back to Stonyhurst (it was during the War), Charles Plater had become the great noise at Oxford as Master of Campion Hall. He went about with a marvelous bulldog which all the wounded Tommies loved. And these Tommies, whether Catholic or not, came pouring into Campion Hall just to see and be with Father Plater.

Plater had a marvelous gift of making you do exactly what he wanted. There's a story told about him and the Catholic people of North Oxford. They were very highbrow. (You can imagine how the wives of dons and people who've settled into the university life at Oxford are apt to become very critical of the Church: they complain about how poorly things are done, the lack of interesting sermons, and so on.) Well, the group at that time formed a circle immediately when they found that Plater was arriving, and waited upon him as soon as he was settled in. You see, he was rector of the church as well as Master of the Jesuit house, and they intended to tell him exactly what they wanted done. A person who was there told me the meeting was very amusing. At the end of it, as you watched the scene, these people had committed themselves to do all sorts of things for the Catholic Social Guilds, and Plater had not committed himself to a single one of their proposals!

Let me give you an example of another facet of Father Plater's character: his kindness and selflessness. At about the time that he came on as Master of Campion Hall, C.C. Martindale became very ill and had pretty much of a complete collapse. It was just before his ordination, and he was then sent over to Dublin to the theological house there. He spent most of his time in his fourth year with the sick in the hospitals, just living with them all the time, completely. He was so sick that he was never able to do his points at his final examination. Then everything was against him when he came back to England (what with the criticism of a book he had written and all that), and he was sent just to coach at Stonyhurst. There, he wrote one or two of his rather more pessimistic books. About this time Charles Plater said to me, "You're going up to Stonyhurst. Do you think Martindale would like to come here? Would you find out?" You see, he knew of my intimacy with Father Martindale. Well, when I asked Martindale he replied, "I'm not interested." But I told Father Plater to invite him anyway and, sure enough, he accepted. When he arrived, Charles Plater, who'd been the great noise there at Oxford, stepped aside and passed to Martindale all the most interesting and wonderful persons, keeping for himself the uninteresting ones. Gradually he pushed Martindale into a position of prominence. When I came back to Oxford a year later, Martindale was beginning to expand and grow and get back all his wonderful mental acuity and vitality and zest. In fact, by then he was being talked about in Oxford, and Father Plater was receding into the background—like John the Baptist, you see. And Plater said to me, "Father, will you just find out if there is anything Father Martindale wants. If there's anything I can do for him, would you tell me? I don't feel I should ask him myself; but if you find anything he wants, let me know." Now, to my mind, this bordered on the heroic. If Plater had been a vain man, he would have tried to keep some position for himself. What did he do? He surrendered everything to Martindale. It was because he was such a lovely man in this and in so many other ways that everybody who knew him loved him.

Early in life, in his forties, fully spent, never having spared himself but really killing himself with work, he finally agreed to go out to Malta with a beloved doctor friend for a rest. It was a small, rather Catholic place at the time.

He almost brought it to complete life again in a matter of days. Within a week he was the best-known man there. And he was just going into a house one day when he suddenly fell over dead. They had a complete national funeral for him even though he'd been there only a week.

I mentioned Father Martindale just now, when speaking of Charles Plater. He is surely one of the outstanding converts within living memory. Some hold he stands at the very top of the list. It was only last year that Father Harold Gardiner, who is now the literary editor of *America* but was doing a semester at Georgetown at the time, told me, "You know, Father Philip Hughes, the historian, maintains that the greatest convert to Catholicism in England since Newman is Father Martindale." I accept that in a way, but would have to weigh it carefully because I just might be inclined to put Father Gerard Manley Hopkins above Martindale.

C.C. Martindale was the son of Sir Arthur Martindale, who was knighted out of the Indian Civil Service. He went to Harrow and Stonyhurst. When he came into the Church and joined the Jesuits, he was a young man of astonishing ability and outstanding reputation. He went up to Oxford and got Firsts in Moderation and in Greats; in addition he won nearly every possible academic prize and scholarship. Amazingly brilliant.

I was quite young when I first came into contact with him and I started off with absolute crazy worship for him. In my days at Stonyhurst, after the end of secondary school, one could take a two-year course as a gentleman philosopher. While you did a course in philosophy, you lived the life of a country gentleman. It was a very enjoyable life indeed. Well, Martindale had arrived back at Stonyhurst, having just finished Oxford, and he was teaching in the school. I'd heard people say that this was a most astonishingly brilliant young Jesuit, and I still remember how I was struck by him. Then, when I decided I would become a Jesuit and went to be a novice, Martindale had been sent from Stonyhurst to the house of studies to teach the juniorate. I had nothing much to do there, except pray and study a bit, and I used to stare at this man and think how simply marvelous he was. It was at this time that I first got to know him.

Then, when I took my vows, they said I was to stay on for a year and needn't do the ordinary juniorate studies. Archbishop Goodier (he was Father Goodier at the time) was head of the juniorate, and he said, "You just read and do Latin and Greek. And I suggest that you do Latin verse for Mr. Martindale." So I started off by sending him copies of Latin verse. Well, I would get back wonderful great foolscap pages covered with the most brilliant versions. For instance, I'd take a piece of Tennyson or Wordsworth or somebody like that, put it into Latin verse, and send it off; then I'd discover from the verses Martindale would send back just what Wordsworth or Tennyson was talking about. I'd never got these lights upon these poets before. You see, Martindale would do about five or six versions for me, all so brilliant and lovely. I'd think, "My goodness, the word *in* took the accusative there." And then he'd suddenly put at the end of a letter, "I can't stand the food we're having at dinner today, so I'm writing this during the meal. I'm sorry, because the cabbage will spoil some of the effects." And off would come some remarkable piece. Well, that was Martindale. He was really an astonishing person.

But then his health broke down completely just as he finished his theology. The story is told (I don't know whether it's true) that the doctor said to him, "Look here, you've exhausted practically every piece of nervous fibre you have. You've got nervous exhaustion. If you go on like this, you'll either die or end up in the madhouse. I think it would be much better if you left the Jesuits." But Martindale said, "Oh, no, I'll stay on. I'll risk death or madness, but I will remain."

But there he was, terribly ill, and about that same time he had a very unhappy experience. I cannot vouch for this, but I have heard it from several sources. After Martindale left Oxford he began to write rapidly. Among other things, he wrote a life of St. John the Apostle. Well, there was a Father Drum (General Hugh Drum's brother, I believe) who was professor of theology at Fordham. When this life of St. John came out, Father Drum read it and said it was heretical, abominable, tainted with modernism and had to be denounced. Apparently he or someone else must have written to Rome. Well, at this period modernism was rather strong, you see, and when this accusation was brought against Martindale, this whole question of whether he was a modernist or not made it a most difficult time for him. It upset and depressed him dreadfully. I am told that he couldn't write even a postcard without having it censored. I am sure the accusation was completely false, but he was under this cloud of suspicion of being heretically minded; and that, it is said, stood in the way, first, of his inclination to come to the United States and, second, of his being invited. That's the period of his pessimism to which I referred in connection with Father Charles Plater. But after his return to Oxford, he came into his own, though his health continued to remain uncertain. For example, when one of his scholarship prizes demanded that he should bring out a special text in the Oxford version of Ausonius, he had to give it up.

It was at this stage, apparently, that he decided to turn from scholarship and live just for the simple people, like those in the East End and the Tommies and the policemen and the pugilists. By this time he had discovered that he had this great magnetism for them, you see; he embarked upon this extraordinary life which he's gone on doing. He has a strange but amazing vitality—sick half the year, but recovering so well between times that he is able to do the most prodigious things.

He was constantly ill. He'd have a temperature of 102° or 103° in the morning, and everybody would say he was about to go and should have the Last Sacraments. Then in the afternoon he'd be as well as could be, as right as rain. At night he'd be there pounding on the piano until twelve o'clock with a group of tough East End boys all gathered around him and just adoring him. Martindale's really a most extraordinary man: he has a tremendous genius, is gigantically spiritual and at the same time has a real flair for attracting people—almost a magnetism. In his room, the walls were completely adorned with photographs from the oddest people—from tough boxers, watermen, seamen.

While I would not say Martindale is a wit, he does have quite a sense of humor. He was sitting in a train once reading his Office, when two men got in. One of them glanced at him and said, "By Jove, a bloody parson!" Martindale, without looking up, said, "Bloody, eh?" And the man said, "Well, I'm damned!" To which Martindale replied, "Not yet," and went on reading his Office! That story was told to Lord Northcliffe, who was supposed to have enjoyed it enormously.

It would be impossible to list all the things Martindale has done. He started the whole of the Inter-University Movement; he was a considerable scripture scholar; he was a Latin and Greek scholar; he wrote essays and stories; he wrote a whole series of biographies of his friends: Robert Hugh Benson, Bernard Vaughan, Charles Plater, Roy Steuart. Speaking of those particular biographies, I must say that, to my way of thinking, none of them are really good. They treat the men rather poorly, take them down a bit. Though Father Martindale loved writing these lives, every time he wrote one the man seemed to come out an inferior creature. Charles Plater was a much greater man than the Martindale biography would have him. I lost my completely uncritical worship of Martindale when I read that book.

I do hope I haven't denigrated him by what I have just said, because—although I think he has got certain curiosities to him—he unquestionably has a tremendous genius.

One of the curious things about him is the way other people took over things at which he was supreme before people recognized he really was so good. For example, he was the person who created a whole new way of writing lives of saints. Before him, there were just the old pious books about saints. Then Martindale wrote about them, saint after saint. He wrote of them as *Captains of Christ, Soldiers of Christ,* all alive, very natural and human and so understandable. In a way, even Father Brodrick has stolen his thunder. Although Martindale is a much greater genius than Brodrick (as Father Brodrick would be the first to admit, I think), yet Brodrick has become far better known (at least in the United States, I believe) than Martindale for his biographies of saints—even though Martindale started all that. Again, he was the great scripture scholar, and there Ronald Knox has acquired the reputation. Also, he was the man who started off the volumes entitled *The History of Religions* which were published by the Catholic Truth Society. This was an enormously important work in those days when the West was becoming interested in the new religions of the East: what Hinduism was, what Buddhism was, what Taoism was, and all the rest. At a time when it was said that Christianity was only a slightly different form of other religions, Father Martindale had these volumes brought out. And they are very valuable still. So now other people are taking the credit for things he really created, you see: the interest in the lives of the saints, the interest of Catholics in the universities, many things on scriptural study, on comparative religion.

He's never written any philosophical works. I wouldn't say that he was philosophically inclined generally. His is a tremendously intelligent mind, but I don't think he will be remembered for philosophical contributions. If you were to ask me, considering how great a person he is, what work he would be remembered by, I'm not sure I could give you the answer. There were slighter books when he was young, which all youth adored—things like *Unchanging Nacidemon* and, I think, *Waters of Twilight,* which was a book of stories, marvelous stories. They had enormous influence in their day but are forgotten now, I'm afraid.

So there is Father C.C. Martindale, a true genius. Now he's eighty-two, but he's still producing. For example, he brought out a new text of the scriptures for the schools last year. He's always doing something new! His mind is as active as ever, though they say his body is getting feeble. What nearly killed him was that he went over to lecture in Denmark in 1939, about a fortnight before war broke out, and was caught there for the duration. He had to live in Denmark in the bitter cold, without proper treatment. He was already a sick man and terribly sensitive to cold, and he used to have about three stoves in his room to keep him alive and going. And he developed false angina. But that was 1941, twenty years ago; and, as I say, he's still producing, though now living in semi-retirement at one of our houses outside London.

Another remarkable Jesuit of the old days whom I knew rather well was Father Herbert Thurston. He was born in the Channel Islands, either in Jersey or Guernsey. (The English know almost nothing about these islands except that you escape taxes by living there. Incidentally, the French Jesuits have a house of studies there.) Herbert Thurston was profoundly English, with an intensely skeptical mind. Early on, I think, he made up his mind that he was not going into philosophy or theology, that they were too dangerous as subjects. When the modernist crisis came on and Father Tyrrell (who had been a great friend of his) left the Society and the Church and then became an agnostic of sorts, Father Thurston must have been confirmed in his own decision. When he discovered that Tyrrell had been writing under an assumed name while he was a Jesuit, he was dreadfully upset. A man of such uprightness himself, he simply couldn't understand how a man could be a member of the Society, fed and nurtured by it and living in it as an open Catholic, and then write articles against it under an assumed name. He was a magnificently loyal man and he regarded it as a most treacherous thing. The whole Tyrrell incident, I think, darkened the world for Thurston. More than ever before, he settled down to becoming an historian. It was as though he had said to himself, "When you write history, you're relating facts and not delivering opinions. So long as you keep to the facts, you're all right."

Farm Street Church

There were several very interesting priests in the Farm Street community in Father Thurston's day. In fact, it was truly a most remarkable community at that particular period. There was wonderful Father Roy Steuart, a glorious person, a splendid figure of a man, and extremely witty. Descended from Scotch kings, he'd been in the artillery before he became a Jesuit. He was the kind of man who wrote lovely books on mysticism but at the same time also adored boxing. There was the then young Father Martindale. And a Father Keating—who had an ardent Irish patriotism, although he talked with a most exquisite English accent—was quite interesting in his own way, too. And one must not forget Father Francis Woodlock, one of my greatest friends. He loved teasing people. It was very amusing to watch him tease Father Martindale or Father Thurston. They would become very prim, entirely cold, and could see nothing funny at all in his teasing. It is interesting to note that Thurston is said to have written a humorous limerick on Father Bernard Vaughan that went something like this:

A holy ascetic named Vaughan
Came to pray in the church before dawn;
Each deeply drawn sigh
Might, he thought, edify;
But the people said, "Lord, what a yawn!"

Mind you, Father Martindale had a wonderful sense of humour, and so did Father Thurston, but they didn't like that form of personal joking. That's one of the differences, I think, between an Irish temperament and an English one.

Well, Thurston was in this community and he did extraordinarily valuable research work. He was always at the British Museum and was constantly uncovering interesting documents. He was supposed to have more knowledge of the files and cards and books of the Museum than even its curators. He did an immense lot of work on the liturgy of the Church and on the saints. He helped, for instance, to rewrite the whole of Butler's *Lives of the Saints,* in twelve volumes. Innumerable pieces of his work are still held extremely valuable.

At one point he had a lamentable experience with a man named G.G. Coulton. This man had written numerous volumes on medieval times. He hated the Church with a passion and simply couldn't believe that Catholics were not hypocrites and wrongheaded and deceitful. As a result, no matter what you said, he just went on saying you were a liar. On one occasion he attacked Father Thurston; and after that, Thurston couldn't get rid of him. Whatever he said, Coulton twisted it wrong, you see. Once, Father Thurston reviewed, I think, one of the great Protestant books by a man at Trinity—I forget what it was on. At any rate, in his review Father Thurston said the book was full of mistakes. Immediately Coulton wrote in and challenged him and said, "I defy you to find one mistake in any particular chapter." So Thurston replied very quietly, "I think I could find for you five or more mistakes in any single *page* of the book you'd like to select." So then they chose an arbitrator on this matter, the great philosopher G.E. Moore. Thurston thereupon found in the page chosen, not five mistakes, but ten or twelve. With that he closed out the controversy. But not so for Coulton, who went on to say for the rest of his life that Thurston had lied and pretended, had withdrawn, had feared to face him, and wouldn't go on with the argument. That was very tiring on Father Thurston, but that was Coulton's way, always.

Herbert Thurston spent, I would suppose, fifty years or more at Farm Street. He was a splendid and active spiritual adviser before he turned his efforts to study and to writing. Then he became a most prolific writer—books, pamphlets, articles. He was a constant contributor to our magazine, *The Month,* and wrote countless articles for encyclopedias. He was also one of the foremost Catholic controversialists of his day. (It was there that he met up with Coulton.) Toward the end of his life, he developed an interest in strange phenomena, psychical and physical, like stigmata, elevation from the ground, cases of people who apparently lost height and weight and were reduced to much smaller size, and so on. Thurston was very careful not to say that any of these had spiritual implications. He merely went to the British Museum and other places where there were libraries to find reports, gather them together, grade the evidence, make it into a scientific article and then present it, you see. His papers were interesting because they were so carefully and quietly and unprejudicedly produced.

Father Thurston was also very interested in poltergeists. He couldn't seem to make up his mind about them at all. They puzzled him because the evidence he produced by his research was so astonishing. I can remember an instance when one of my own Jesuits, on his way to Rome, wrote me a letter from Paris saying he had come across a man who was a stigmatic. He enclosed photographs of stigmata on this man's hands and said his name was Morasco. About three or four months afterwards, I happened to come into the recreation room on Farm Street one day and heard Father Thurston mention the name Morasco. So I came up and said, "Oh, Father Thurston, that's very interesting. I heard you mention a man named Morasco.," And Thurston said, "It's not a him; it's a her, a woman. A very interesting case. She was a Belgian girl. She had a kind of hysterical stigmatization when she was about twelve or fourteen and got everybody interested. The clergy and the bishop, they all believed in her. She insisted on being taken to a holy well someplace and she was finally cured. Apparently it was a complete case of hysteria. When she grew up and the war broke out, she thought she'd dress as a man. So she did and started to wear a uniform. Then she claimed to have the stigmata again, but recently she's been put into a prison for embezzlement." Now, that was typical of Thurston, knowing the critical details on some remote person.

There is a story that one of the Provincials was dying and Thurston came into his room to ask for a blessing, and the old priest spoke up and said, "Herbert, Herbert, one last prayer before I die: will you please leave us the Trinity?" He was so devastating in his criticism, you see. But he was a lovely man, possessed of immense integrity, and you could always rely on him. But his most remarkable characteristic was this phenomenal talent for getting facts.

I remember somebody once said to me that the Holy Roman Church put such a premium on its religious being unmarried that there were hardly any married saints. And at that particular moment I couldn't think of even one. When I came back to Farm Street to lunch, there was Father Thurston picking at his food. So I said, "Oh, Father, can you tell me if there are any married saints?" "Well," he said, "there's so-and-so and so-and-so," ticking off name after name from memory. Then off he went to his work. He was unbelievable in those ways. He could always give you the facts. It was wonderful to have such a man in the community because, whenever there was a difficulty, you always went to him, and he'd somehow dredge up out of his enormous knowledge some fact that would just suit what you wanted.

Father Stephen McNamee at Georgetown tells a story that again illustrates this point. It seems he went over to London to Farm Street in his early days as a young Jesuit. When he was seated at the table the first night, somebody asked him what he was over there for. He explained that he was supposed to write a paper on some rather little-known philosopher, some man practically nobody had ever heard of. At that, Father Thurston, who was across the table, lifted his head and said, "Oh, you mean So-and-So?" Then he gave about fifteen minutes of commentary covering absolutely everything Father McNamee had discovered after a great deal of research, thinking it was all original work. And Father Thurston had it all in the back of his mind!

People loved him very much because he was so good and so fine. Again, I don't think he knew what fear was. His strength of will was gigantic. We have a school at Beaumont, near Windsor, about twenty miles outside London. I'm told Father Thurston, when he was a young man, would just walk there—the whole twenty miles—to say Mass, starting out about three or four in the morning. Even in his later seventies, he would walk up into Hampstead (which was about three or four miles, I suppose, and mostly uphill) to say Mass in the morning. He was very fond of a private nursing home there. I think he'd had something to do with founding it, though I don't know for certain. At any rate, he'd very often walk up there to say Mass.

Not long before he died at the age of eighty-two or three, he began to fail. I wasn't there, but I'm told that one day he went to one of the side altars at Farm Street to say Mass, and, as he descended the steps to say the opening blessing, suddenly down he went. His heart was failing him, and he went down in this dead faint. So people rushed up the center aisle and tended him. Slowly he came to, looked at them, brushed them aside, struggled to his feet and started, *"In nomine Patris, et Filii, et Spiritus Sancti. Amen. Introibo ad altare Dei."* A most wonderful man.

Belloc, Chesterton and Baring

Hilaire Belloc is not much read these days but, I have no doubt about it, he will come back. He wrote such beautiful poetry, such superb prose, and both so moving! He was one of the great men of his time. I myself always think of him as one of the biggest figures I ever met.

Although Belloc pretended to be French, he was really three-quarters English, his father having been half-French and half-English and his mother English. But he did do his military service as a soldier in the French Army, and this was what made him so well acquainted with all the terrain of France. During the First World War, he was *the* authority on what was happening. He knew the battlefields. It was like walking over his garden. He had an immense and exact sense of territory and places in France. On his mother's side he was descended from, I think, one of the great English scientific discoverers. As a boy he was sent to the Oratory School, which had been founded by Newman. It was a very aristocratic school in a way, because Newman's friends, like the Norfolks and the Scotts and the Wards, all sent their sons there. Belloc remembers Newman coming into the schoolroom in his great old age as a Cardinal.

After the Oratory, Belloc went up to Balliol. At that time, Oxford had a remarkably brilliant set of men. There was F.E. Smith (who wasn't Balliol), who became Lord Birkenhead, Lord Chancellor of England. He was a brutal, ambitious type of man, but an amazingly able and brilliant person who left his mark on the law and, indeed, on the country. Then there was Sir John Simon, who again was outstanding. There were many others, including that paragon of beauty and athleticism and everything else, C.B. Fry. In America, of course, you're not likely to have heard of C.B. Fry, but when I was a youngster in England he was—oh, just about everything. He arrived at the University, as handsome as Apollo, a great Latin and Greek scholar, and an astonishing athlete as well. He held the long-jump record at the time, could run the hundred yards in ten seconds, was one of the greatest cricketers of all time, and was an international footballer. I can still remember looking at the cricket scores, and everything was "C.B. Fry." He could have been anything he chose to be. And he lived a long life and died only about three or four years ago.

I am reminded of an incident relating to C.B. Fry. When he got old, people didn't remember at all his personal record as a great athlete and a scholar. They knew him only as a commentator on sports because he used to be chosen to comment on various international matches. Well, there was the "brains trust" on the radio in the old days in England, and this particular program included Bertrand Russell, some commander in the Navy who was a phenomenally learned man, Joad (who again was one of those desperately accurate men), and C.B. Fry. One of the questions asked was, "Who was the first mathematical philosopher?" So the BBC man said, "Oh, this rather suits you, Russell. Will you answer?" "Very good," said Bertrand Russell. "It raises a question, of course, which is rather difficult to answer because most philosophers are mathematicians, but I should say on the whole that the first mathematical philosopher would be Plato." And then the most elegant voice said, "No, no, Russell, I don't think you are right. I should say Pythagoras undoubtedly was the first mathematical philosopher." This was C.B. Fry, you see. And he was completely right, too: Pythagoras had been the founder of mathematical philosophy.

Well, Belloc was with these men at Oxford and had wonderful stories about them. He loved Oxford, and records of the time contain many stories about him: his storming away at the Union, his marvelous oratory against F.E. Smith and Simon and the rest—great battles, his roaring, singing French songs, tearing down the hill on a bicycle, and chanting poems of his own making. An altogether terrific character. He was a very poor man, and he hoped (indeed, expected) to be made a fellow of Balliol and also a fellow of All Souls. But he wasn't chosen. Some said it was because he was a Catholic, but it may well have been just because they thought him a very odd man. At any rate, he never could get over that, and it remained the wound in his life all his days. Then matters were made worse when, a year or two after, they appointed as a don at Balliol a man whom he despised. This was "Sligger" Urquhart, a very cultured Catholic man, but not of the stature of Belloc at all. I say this even though I was very fond of Urquhart personally.

Everybody accused Belloc of being a French bourgeois, rather avaricious, close on pennies and in fact preoccupied with the idea of money. Indeed, he annoyed Father Robert Gannon terribly when he arrived to give lectures at Fordham a good many years ago. Financial arrangements had been fixed in advance, but Belloc arrived and shuffled in and said: "How do you do? How do you do? I've brought my secretary with me and I expect, of course, you will take care of her board and keep and fee, too." Father Gannon was simply enraged. He felt, I think, that a man doing business wants business done, and this seemed outrageous. He finally decided to pay the secretary but only on condition that Belloc hand over his lectures to be published by Fordham Press.

Why was Belloc so concerned about money? There's no doubt that he was French in that respect, but he was also a very generous man in many ways. The difficulty was family expenses. He had three children. One was married to a man who ran a prep school; and when this son-in-law became a Catholic, he had to give that up, you see, and Belloc had to find, say, seven hundred fifty pounds a year for a son; and he had a second daughter, who wrote poetry and to whom he gave another two hundred fifty pounds. So he had to find each year some twelve hundred pounds before he could begin to provide for himself, and this question of money did become rather an obsession with him, there's no doubt about that. As a result, he took to writing a lot of potboilers, and this did a great disservice to his reputation.

Now let me tell you a story to show Belloc's generosity. I was going to lunch one day with Lady de Vesci's daughter, Mary Herbert, who had a house not far from Farm Street, and Belloc joined us. It was a Sunday, I remember, and Belloc asked me, "Father, do you know a Miss Walsh?" I replied, "No, why do you ask me?" And he said, "I was at Mass at Farm Street this morning and, as I was leaving church, a woman came up and began talking to me. So I asked her, 'Madam, who are you? What do you want?' And she answered, 'My name is Miss Walsh and I want twenty pounds.' To which I exclaimed, 'My God, Madam, I don't believe I've got that much in the world!' " So, after much laughter, I asked Belloc, "Well, what happened? What did you do?" And he said, "Oh, I gave her the twenty pounds!" Now, you see, that's not the action of a man so obsessed with money that he was a miser.

And what a lovely tale is Belloc's love of his wife! He fell in love with this American girl from California, but she apparently wanted to become a nun. So just when he had finished as an undergraduate at Oxford, or at any rate when he was quite young and had no money, he managed to work his way across the Atlantic and right across the United States to California—all this to persuade her to marry him. Eventually they were married and they had absolute bliss. But she died quite young. The children were still very small, and Belloc was a melancholy man for the rest of his life. He just lived by the Faith after that.

His poetry is so beautiful and it's got all that melancholy in it. And much of his prose is superb, too. I myself am moved by both his prose and poetry. It is really quite stirring and lovely.

The Path to Rome is regarded as one of Belloc's best. I don't myself care for it very much, but most people—ninety percent of his admirers—like it immensely. I quite agree there are lovely parts in it. There are truly wonderful songs and bursts of music. But I do not feel the book is Belloc's best work, much less one of the great works of literature. What I regarded as the great work of Belloc are those passages of beautiful description in historical scenes, and again those passages where he just bursts into merriment. An example would be the passage which ends, "There are two great boats that have been created by God and man—one is the Ark and the other is the *Nona,* and the greater of the two is the *Nona.*" (He loved boating, and the *Nona* was his boat.) It is all so magnificent.

Robert Speaight has very nearly, but not quite, done Belloc justice in his biography. I would add to that book the one by the other man who knew him so well, Johnny Morton. Morton, Wyndham Lewis, Douglas Woodruff—those who loved Belloc thought the world of him, really adored him. Women adored him, too: Diana Cooper and Katherine Asquith, for example. And all that tremendous group of young geniuses of England who were all killed in the First World War, the Julian Grenfells and the rest, loved him and referred to him in their letters. He was such a character, really such a character, and such a lovely person in his way. He had a tremendous personality. You couldn't get away from him. And, as I say, somehow everything he did and said was in character.

I must own he could be a very difficult man. I used to entertain him occasionally, usually a bit frightened because I never knew what mood he would be in or what he would say. At dinner he might say, "Oh, I don't care for this food." He liked to be thought very courteous, had a great view on courtesy, and wrote a poem on it. But he didn't realize that when he was very moody he was anything but courteous! I think you'll find that very frequently happens with men who have enormous independence and personality. They do not realize the devastating effect their words and actions sometimes have on people. Think of some others who have had that marvelous tang and tremendous character: the Duke of Wellington, Samuel Johnson. They are personalities you can't escape from. You see, they're so alive. They enter a room, and everybody is immediately aware of them.

Now, Belloc was not a man who appealed to everyone. I wouldn't for a moment say that he would have had the same effect on everyone as he had on me. I think he was a very great man, but I admit that he had the defects of his personality. That so often happens. It is surely true with priests.

One can meet crusty priests who are geniuses; and some you find very attractive even so, and some you don't.

One facet of Belloc that is often overlooked was his profound learning. It made him a most dangerous antagonist in discussion or debate. I'll give you two examples of that.

One was when the chaplaincy at Oxford was enlarged, and Ronald Knox asked Belloc to come and speak at the big evening gathering. (You see, the old chaplaincy was a former bishop's palace, a lovely place, but not large enough for the undergraduates; so they built an extension onto it and, at the opening, had this evening affair.) In his talk Belloc came out with one his pet themes: that the Anglo-Saxons were utterly unimportant in the history of England. Now, there was present on this occasion a man who was probably the greatest authority in the world on Anglo-Saxon subjects and was the professor of Anglo-Saxon history at the time. He is presently professor of English Literature at Oxford. This man's name was Tolkien, and he was a very good Catholic. (Incidentally, he wrote a book of fairy tales called *The Hobbit*. It is a pure work of genius. In it Tolkien creates a whole new type of being. In a way, it's an allegory of life.)

Well, Tolkien disagreed profoundly with Belloc on this question of the Anglo-Saxons. He was sitting just in front of me, and I saw him writhing as Belloc came out with some of his more extreme remarks. So during the interval, I said to him, "Oh, Tolkien, now you've got your chance. You'd better tackle him." He looked at me and said, "Gracious me!

Do you think I would tackle Belloc unless I had my whole case very carefully prepared?" He knew Belloc would always pull some fact out of his sleeve which would disconcert you! Now, that was a tremendous tribute from probably the greatest authority in the world at the time on that particular subject.

The second example involves a story that was told to me by a third person, but I believe it to be quite true. Belloc was once lecturing at Cambridge, and when the questions started, a very tall, gaunt and gawky figure asked him a question. Belloc probably recognized who the man was, but at any rate he turned to the chairman and asked, "Who is this fool?"

Now, the questioner was the famous C.G. Coulton, who was such a plague to Catholics and did infinite damage by his books. He challenged all the beautiful legends about the goodness of the medieval monks and friars, and raked up every scandal possible. You see, he had this gigantic array of facts taken from all sources and all periods and, unfortunately, he would put them all together—whether they were from the twelfth century or the fourteenth—in order to deceive people. With his enormous knowledge of the Middle Ages, he virtually destroyed Cardinal Gasquet in a controversy, and went on to do battle with Belloc, Chesterton, Arnold Lunn, Herbert Thurston (as I mentioned earlier), and many other Catholics. And he never knew when he was defeated: he just went on and on, slamming you even though you had demolished him utterly in fact and in logic. He was a most dreadful man.

Well, Coulton overheard this remark of Belloc's—as Belloc might well have intended that he should—and immediately dipped down and took out of his folder a large piece of paper. I suppose it had on it all the errors Belloc had ever made in his writings. And Coulton said to the chairman, "May I ask Mr. Belloc why, in writing a book on the Battle of Evesham, he quotes as an authority Matthew of Paris, who died fifteen years before that battle took place?" Now, that looked pretty bad for Belloc, but he immediately bounced up and said, "Any fool knows that there is an appendix which goes by the name of Matthew Paris which was written *after* the Battle of Evesham and which is quoted under the name of Matthew of Paris." That shows what a knowledgeable sort of man Belloc was.

He had an astonishing gift of clarity, of getting on to the exact point of an important issue. While he wasn't technically a philosopher, if you were discussing a philosophical point with him you'd probably find he was most illuminating. I can give you an example again of that.

Sir Esme Howard had a very nice son, Hubert, who was inclined to take himself and his work rather seriously. Now, at one time he'd been out in Munich consulting some Benedictine on Kantian philosophy. So when he next met Belloc, he proceeded rather to bore Hilaire by telling him all about this Benedictine and how important Kant was and how people didn't realize his importance. Belloc listened patiently and finally, when young Hubert paused for breath, he said, "My boy, the truth of the matter is this..." And then he summed up Kant and his philosophical weaknesses just like that. Now, that shows a very remarkable gift.

Belloc listened attentively in the case I have quoted, but I don't know as I would say he was a good listener, any more than I'd say he was generally a patient man. But there again, I think he probably could have exercised superb patience in a crisis. Of course, his health could have affected his patience. He was not a well man. Though he looked like a sea captain, and risked his body on the water and in great walking tours, he did become rather feeble in body as he grew older. But he was always a very vibrant and wonderful person. When he was in form, the songs he could sing—with that lovely tenor voice! I loved his songs and the merriment and the glory and happiness that would exude from him. He could positively intoxicate people. He could be enchanting in conversation, too. On the whole, he was kind, using his wit not to hurt too much. He never paid any attention to what other people were thinking about him, had no sense of human respect whatsoever. As a result he always acted just as he felt, and the mood he was in came out, sometimes with disastrous effects upon people. I'll tell you a story on that point. It resulted almost in the ruin of relations between Catholics in America and Catholics in England.

When Esme Howard was our ambassador to the United States, one of his great desires was to bring closer together the Catholics of the United States and those of England. He knew Father James Gillis and knew that he headed some kind of movement—called some name like "Pilgrims"—

composed of Catholics who used to go to Rome every year. So Esme Howard arranged with them that, instead of going to Rome this particular year, they should go to England. Well, Howard formed a committee (I remember because I was on it) to see how we could make things as pleasant as possible for these American Catholic pilgrims. Everything was done for them: there was a tour of London and a visit to Oxford, the police of London arranged to clear the streets so that they could go up to the Tower of London without any difficulty, the Duke of Norfolk opened his Arundel castle for them. They had an hilarious and wonderful week. And it was at the banquet which was to climax the visit that disaster happened.

At this banquet Father Gillis got up and made a very eloquent talk. Very moved by all the hospitality, he spoke about the ties between English and American Catholics, how they joined together, and all the rest. Now, Belloc had been asked to make the reply speech. But the evening had not been going very well for him. The food had not been to his taste, and he had started ordering special dishes. And he wasn't in his good mood at all. So he got to his feet and started right off by saying, "The first thing one's got to remember is that there's no more relation between the American Catholic and the English Catholic than there is between the Laplander and the Hottentot." Then he proceeded to develop his thesis. Well, the effect was disastrous! And Douglas Woodruff, who is the editor of *The Tablet* and was to second the reply, worsened matters by making an unfortunate decision: he concluded he might be able to turn the tide by making the situation humorous, and so he proceeded to attempt to do so. But the American gentlemen already were so indignant and hurt that it only rubbed in the salt. As for Father Gillis, he swore he would never again have anything whatsoever to do with English Catholics. And from that day you can date, I believe, the animosity which appeared in his writings in *The Catholic World,* the constant bitterness towards England and Englishmen—all caused by my beloved Belloc. I think of him as the Samuel Johnson of our age. You see, when Samuel Johnson wasn't in the mood, my goodness, he must have been a horror. The things he would say! But what a great man he was when all is said and done: one of the greatest figures in literature, as Boswell has shown him.

Belloc simply was indifferent to the rest of the world. Yet he loved people and was very deeply attached to his friends. There are his lovely lines which I murmur in my old age constantly: (Apart from the love of God) "There's nothing worth the wear of winning but laughter and the love of friends." Those lines are so moving to me.

I remember a story told by a charming lady whom I myself knew only casually but who was a great friend of Belloc's. It has always stayed in my mind because it seemed to me somehow quite complete. She said that she'd once been over in Dieppe and happened to be passing down the esplanade when she looked into a restaurant window and saw Hilaire Belloc sitting at a table by himself. Knowing Belloc, she felt frightened about just going in and speaking to him;

so she called a waiter and said, "Would you see if I can speak to Mr. Belloc?" A moment or two later the waiter came back with the terse reply, "Mr. Belloc says that he knows no woman in Dieppe." It was a great phrase, somehow or other. Then she took her courage in her hands and just went up to him. Of course, when he saw who she was, he threw his arms around her.

I think in a certain sense I'm a hero worshiper, and I worshiped Belloc in a way. I believe I see his faults and I feel that some of the people who thought so highly of him exaggerated his good qualities, but I still feel that he was an immense personality. He was a tremendous Catholic and used his splendid talents in the service of God. But he labored under great difficulties, disappointed hopes, the early loss of his wife, lack of money, ill health and melancholia.

(In this connection I just wonder if everyone who tries to do something for God doesn't have some unusual cross to carry, and some are equal to it while others are not. Some people surmount their difficulty so well that you don't see their wounds; others show their wounds but carry on nevertheless; and others simply collapse. This is a theory that just occurred to me. I don't know whether it would stand up, but I think it probably would.)

People are always comparing Belloc with Chesterton, you know, and it is a difficult comparison to make. I, for one, do not straightaway concede the higher niche to Chesterton. I often say of Chesterton that God must have been looking the other way when he was conceived, because you'd think the man didn't have any original sin in him. He did talk about having dreadful evil images, but I fancy those were just childish. He didn't really know what evil was. Chesterton remained to his dying day a beloved genius still something of a child. There was always a certain innocence about him.

This great, enormous, three-hundred-pound man would roll about on the floor playing with little children. There was an unwritten law that if any child called at Beaconsfield, where he lived, they were to be immediately admitted. And all writing and everything else was forgotten while the children would clamber about his neck and roll about the floor with him, and he simply roared with laughter, enjoying it thoroughly. Again, he couldn't make an enemy. Everybody felt he was a likeable person. He could say sharp things occasionally, but not often, because he was full of charity.

Chesterton was much more affectionate (or should I say gentle?) than Belloc. But Chesterton would himself have said that he owed a great deal to Belloc. He would have maintained, "I'm only a journalist. I know nothing. My ideas are borrowed from Belloc, then I adorn them and write about them in my own way." He did transfigure them with this extraordinary gift that he had. He was a real genius. But the material, much of it, *did* come from Belloc, for Chesterton himself was not a scholar or even really a reader.

Chesterton, of course, had this amazing gift of picking the core out of a book in no time. He wrote a book on St. Thomas Aquinas, and when I read it I must confess (this

119

sounds conceited, but I hope it isn't) I had the impression that the only book on Aquinas he'd looked at was one I had written. He must have at least glanced at it, because he does take a page disagreeing with something I said in my book, though there's no direct evidence that he ever read it. But this sheer gift of his of picking up something in St. Thomas that was really very vital and important was definitely there.

Chesterton I do regard as a pure genius though he is very much out of fashion now. I'm constantly coming across sneers at him in reviews and periodicals. But what I also notice is that very frequently, when someone wants to make a point in a very sharp saying, he will say, "As G.K. Chesterton said..." You see, they can't keep away from him.

Maurice Baring is, of course, the other person whom people associate with Belloc and Chesterton. The Barings were a great banking family, and in the course of time they acquired two or three titles. One of them was Lord Revelstoke. They came originally, I think, from Germany in the seventeenth or early eighteenth century. They were like the Rothschilds but never reached the riches or the reputation of the Rothschilds.

Maurice Baring went to Eton, then on to Cambridge, and later transferred, I think, for a year to Oxford. He became a convert round about that time, as I recall. Then he grew tremendously fond of Belloc and Chesterton, and they formed the great trio. There is quite a well-known conversation painting of the three of them. Baring wrote a number of novels that many competent critics, especially on the continent of Europe, regarded as superbly good—*Daphne Adeane, C,* and several others. I suppose I like *Daphne Adeane* best, although may people preferred *C.* Then he wrote some interesting reminiscences and a history of Russia. He also produced a lovely anthology, with notes about his favorite passages. Again, he wrote volumes of poetry, and some of his odes are absolutely exquisite. He wrote a poem on Bron Lucas (Lord Lucas) which was so splendid that it caused T.E. Lawrence to come and sit at Baring's feet, as it were.

I got to know him through mutual friends, and he was very kind to me. I used to go down once a year and stop with him for a weekend at his place in Rottingdean, about four miles out of Brighton. He never married but he kept this lovely house with a beautiful garden. He had a wonderful couple, a fabulous woman cook and her husband, who was a most marvelous butler. During the latter part of his life, in a fit of austerity (possibly the Baring bank wasn't doing too well at the time), he got rid of them. But the food and the service were marvelous while he had his servants. For those weekends he used to invite two or three of his dearest friends, who usually happened to be very great friends of mine as well: Mrs. Raymond Asquith, Lady Lovat, and others.

Baring had a certain look like Edward VII. He was a biggish man, flushed in complexion, and he got very bald early in life. He was a lovely character, a man of enormous independence, yet a very humble man in many ways. I don't think he knew what fear was. During the First World War, although he didn't look the type of man to take up that kind of thing at all, he was in the Air Force. He had a wonderful sense of humor and was apt to be very mischievous. The more you told Maurice to stop doing a thing, the more he did it. There are all sorts of charming stories told of him.

For example, once he was with another very distinguished convert, Algernon Cecil, who was the grandson of the famous Lord Salisbury. Cecil was a very serious and brilliant man, but a little bit too heavy, too seriously cultured for Maurice, although he was quite cultured himself. In the middle of a rather deep discussion by Cecil on a view of Bismark or something of that kind, Maurice is supposed suddenly to have begun balancing an egg on his head.

He was frequently invited by the Navy to go out on maneuvers in the Mediterranean. They tell the story that he was on some battleship, and the captain of another ship in the squadron invited him to come to lunch. The Navy in those days was just the pink of perfection, you see, and so a pinnace came alongside to pick up Baring, the men holding their oars straight up, all the perfect Royal Navy style. Maurice waited at the rail until the gangway was put out. Then, as the Navy persons were saying, "Careful, sir. Watch your step, sir. Easy does it, sir," he deliberately misjudged his step and plunged into the water. A moment later he popped up, bald head first, grinning broadly at all hands. Immediately the whole of the Royal Navy was brought to bear to get him aboard ship again. That was typical of Baring. He was very mischievous in those ways.

Again, there was a wonderful and rather famous hotel—the Metropole, I think it was—in Brighton, run by a great character. We used to have dinner there with Maurice occasionally. One night somebody bet him (he was in evening clothes, white shirt and tie and top hat) that he wouldn't walk into the sea fully dressed. Well, Maurice immediately got up, put on his top hat, and walked straight out into the sea. That's the kind of man he was. You dared not challenge him to do a thing because he'd do it right off.

Maurice Baring had happen to him three things that I suppose many of us want: he wrote a poem in his sleep, he saw a ghost, and he experienced a miracle.

As to the poem he wrote: he woke up one night having composed a poem in his sleep, so he immediately wrote it down. When he looked at it in the morning, it turned out to be complete nonsense. At the time he told me about it, he giggled and said, "I put it into the center of one of my volumes of verse and no one's ever noticed what nonsense it is." That appeared to give him great pleasure.

The second thing was Baring's ghost. He was returning one evening to his house at Rottingdean when he saw in the distance a man dressed in eighteenth-century garb. He said to himself, "Well, well. There must have been a fancy dress ball on here, and I've not been told a word about it!" Then he suddenly saw the man turn as though into a wall. So he came up to the wall (I suppose he was about twenty or thirty yards behind) and, sure enough, there was nothing but a wall there. However, an old house stretched out behind the wall. He made inquiries and found there had been a murder at that house in the eighteenth century and that its ghost was supposed to walk. It was a very good story because, you see, the appearance of the ghost was completely unexpected. Baring had had no reason to be thinking of ghosts at all.

The third incident was the miracle. Baring said that it occurred when he was in the diplomatic service in Moscow. His family had been keeping him, I suppose, on a very strict allowance, and he ran rather short of money; so he sent word to his father, and his father dispatched him some rubles. I may be wrong about the exact figure, but my memory seems to say five hundred rubles. To Baring's dismay, he promptly lost them. He searched everywhere he could think of in his apartment and then (he was either already a convert or near to the Church) he started to pray, I forget to which saint, for help in locating the money. As a last resort he went round to his bank and, although he was quite certain there was no hope, he asked the man behind the counter, "Did I make a deposit of five hundred rubles with you today?" The man said, "No, sir. Indeed, you didn't," then added, "but I do think there's something here for you." So he went away and came back and handed Baring an envelope, and inside the envelope were five hundred rubles. Later Maurice discovered his original five hundred rubles between the two cushions of an armchair in his apartment.

Sad to relate, Baring developed a form of palsy. The disease did not kill him, but he got more and more helpless. He'd get up and then fall down, you know. Finally he became like a child and had to have a nurse looking after him day and night. In the end he couldn't move, and even had to have food put to his lips. He spent his last years with his beloved Lady Lovat up at Beaufort Castle, probably in great sanctity because, a man of supreme independence, he endured his absolute helplessness with such patience.

One of the loveliest things about my beloved Maurice was that he used to go daily to Mass when he could. People would watch him after Mass as he came trundling round the little chapel, with his shaking fingers dropping money into the box where you get candles, you see, and shakily lighting and putting up candles. It was a touching scene.

That was Maurice Baring. He was a lovely man. I only wish I could paint him better. Everybody loved him, and I was very privileged to have known him.

Some Other Friends

Now I would like to speak of several of my friends who belong to the group of Catholic writers who followed Belloc, Chesterton and Baring. Let me start with Arnold Lunn.

Arnold Lunn was the son of a Sir Henry Lunn, who had been a non-conformist minister, a doctor and the creator of a number of interesting and successful ventures, including a travel bureau. He was a very remarkable man, as the fact that he was knighted indicates. Arnold went to Harrow, which is supposed to be the rival of Eton, just as Cambridge is *supposed* to be the rival of Oxford. It's remarkable how many brilliant people went to Harrow. For example, Churchill went there, as did Lord Alexander of Tunis. As I recollect, Arnold wrote a book on the Harrovians—a very celebrated book in its time. After Harrow he went up to Oxford, to Balliol.

Benjamin Jowett was the Master of Balliol at the time, and almost every distinguished person who came to Oxford stopped with him. He was a clergyman, an authority on Plato, a friend of most of England's great personages, an altogether fantastic man. He created the great Balliol—changed the whole character of the place and raised the level of scholarship until Balliol became the last word. Great and charming stories are told of him. He used to bring undergraduates to his breakfast table and, for the most part, they would be absolutely terrified. On the other hand, sometimes there were perky ones. Once, a couple of them were having a discussion about God and, having reached a certain point in the argument, one cried up to Jowett seated at the top of the table: "Master, we're discussing God. What do you think of Him?" And the Master replied, "It's not what *you* think of God, it's what God thinks of *you*."

When Arnold Lunn was at Balliol, the college had that Eton set who were all—except for Ronald Knox—killed in the First War. (In those days there was no conscription, and they all put their names down as volunteers.) They were said to have been probably the most brilliant group of Englishmen who ever turned up at Oxford. It must have been a wonderful galaxy of people—though, I suppose, rather aggravating at times. Julian and Billy Grenfell, giants like most of the rest of them, wrote glorious poems as well. Julian could knock over anybody in boxing, could take his horse over any fence, do a thing on Schopenhauer, and write splendid poetry—altogether astonishing.

Julian and Billy Grenfell's father, Lord Desborough, was something of an unusual person himself and once went over Niagara Falls in a barrel. He was a great oarsman, a magnificent figure of a man, a good Christian. When the boys died, the parents published for private circulation at their own expense stories of their childhood. They were brought up as real Christians, though as youths they tended to be somewhat arrogant. Julian was killed in the war. Desperately wounded, he died a very Christian death, mixed with chanting away the chorus endings of Euripides.

But I want to tell you this story about Arnold Lunn, who belonged, not to the Eton set, but to some other set at the college. He was a great mountain climber, even as a young man, and he had no fear whatsoever. He'd been up a mountain in Wales and had fallen. He would have been killed, but some sort of out-jutting ledge of rock had saved him. He fell on this ledge, one leg badly broken, and lay there in great pain for four hours until he was rescued. (Ever since then, he's had one leg shorter than the other, but he remained one of the great climbers of the world even with that short leg.) Well, he came back to Balliol with his leg all bandaged up. This famous Etonian group was having a dinner, and he strode in and said, "Now, according to your code you can't touch me, I'm a damaged man. But I'm going to tel! you some truths which you won't like. You're a damned supercilious lot. Your arrogance is beyond contempt. Most of us hate you, the way you act." And he went on and on. They all sat there, not touching him. Then he suddenly seized the tablecloth and pulled the whole thing off, dishes, glasses, silver and all. Then Julian Grenfell just lifted him up, carried him out, and quietly deposited him in the quadrangle. That was typically Arnold (he's been a fighter all his life); also, I might say, typically Julian Grenfell!

Arnold never got a degree at Oxford. He was sent down for failing to pass the rudiments of Holy Scripture. That was an examination everyone had to pass, showing the old Christian tradition at the University. (I think this requirement was stopped around 1925 or 1930.) I had to go through it and found it terrifying. You interrupted all your ordinary studies, you see, and had to pass this examination in the New Testament in Greek, if possible; if you couldn't do it in Greek, then at least in English. I'm sorry to say there have been occasions when a supercilious don would say to the assembled undergraduates, "I am expecting all of you to pass this thing, but you Roman Catholics will probably take more time to prepare for the New Testament!" At any rate, we once had a most distinguished man, a Jesuit, who actually failed in it! A terrifying examination, as I said. Well, Arnold Lunn failed it completely. (Incidentally, the remarkable poet, John Benjamin—a contemporary of Evelyn Waugh's who has now produced his whole autobiography in verse—was also sent down for failing the examination on Scriptures.)

I mention this examination and Lunn's failing it because, when he was at the top of his form as a speaker, he was invited back to Oxford to speak. There is a university church called St. Mary's; there Newman preached, there the medieval government sometimes met to hold their parliament, there King Charles prayed. And Arnold Lunn was invited by the vicar there to come and give a talk from the pulpit even though he was by then a Catholic. Now, in Oxford, the ordinary undergraduate gown, which you've got to wear when you go to lectures, comes to about your waist. The boast is that over the centuries they get shorter and shorter, and now they are the most ridiculous things—with little wings on the back. On the other hand, a scholar's gown falls to the knee. So Arnold arrived and went to the vicar and said, "What do I do?" "Well, you go to the pulpit and you preach." Then Arnold asked, "What do I wear?" The vicar said, "You wear your master of arts gown." To which Arnold replied, "I've got no such gown. I failed the examination in the rudiments of the Holy Scriptures and never even received a degree at Oxford. So what *do* I wear?" The vicar looked awfully embarrassed and said, "Well, I suppose you've got to wear an undergraduate's gown." So Arnold came along to Campion Hall and asked me to lend him one, and he went into the pulpit wearing this tiny little thing, with wings, and preached a sermon.

As I have said, he was a born fighter, a man without fear. I think that was his great characteristic. And he was always absorbed in what he was doing, paying no attention to anyone else. I remember an incident that occurred not so very long ago. I am a member of the Athenaeum Club in London. I was just strolling by the club, half intending to go in, when at the window I suddenly saw the face of Arnold Lunn. So I came in and, not having seen him in three or four years, expected some sort of greeting. Instead, he immediately asked, "What do you think about that letter in *The Tablet*? I don't agree with it at all, and I'm going to answer it." It was something to do with Moral Rearmament—some argument which he'd been having. That was Arnold all over.

He had tremendous battles with the same Coulton who tangled with Father Thurston and Belloc. If you want a bedside book, the correspondence between Coulton and Lunn is one of the funniest books in the world. They started off peaceably but ended up with the most outrageous statements. In the end, each called the other a liar. But it makes an admirable book for bed-reading: exciting, amusing, and finally putting you to sleep.

In those days Arnold Lunn was always engaged in fighting somebody. He marched right through the United States hunting out Communists and atheists, drawing them into public debates. He is an excellent fighter on the platform. On the other hand, he is a very absent-minded man. His wife had to get him a steel chain and attach all his keys to it so he couldn't lose them. And the story goes that he lived at a small place outside London, about fourteen stations down the line on one of those electrical railways. When he was completely absorbed in thought about how to answer Coulton or Aldous Huxley or Ronald Knox or somebody else, he'd get out of the train at every station, and the conductor, who knew him well, would just push him back in. When they finally reached his place, then all was well.

Again, he would wander into a Lyons café, where all the cakes and biscuits and cookies are sold and, still thinking how he was going to smash Bertrand Russell or some other antagonist, he'd pick up something and start chewing on it and then walk out again. And they'd rush out and yell after him. He was always in danger of being arrested for taking things without paying for them.

Arnold did several books of battles in correspondence. He did that one with Coulton, of course; he did one with Ronald Knox; and he did one with Haldane. I thought in a way he rather got the better of Ronald Knox. I don't think Ronald really bothered about Arnold, but was just teasing him. Of course, they were very fond of one another and had been at Balliol at the same time, Ronald belonging to that famous set. As a result, when Arnold decided to become a Catholic, he came in terrific excitement up to Oxford, announced himself to Ronald Knox and said, "I'm going to become a Catholic. I want you to receive me." And Knox, according to Arnold, leaned back and said, "God help us. Have I got to do that?" And that cooled him down, you see. I gave Arnold his First Communion; and when he was knighted, only two or three years ago, he rang me up or came around to me and asked me to give him communion again on the morning he was going to receive his knighthood. Rather touching, I thought.

He is really such a splendid man, with far more gifts than generally recognized. He's one of those men who might suddenly send you a book of poetry, and you wouldn't be surprised. He's got a touch of genius, although when he gets on one of his favorite subjects, he's apt to keep on it rather too long. But, as I said, he's a real fighter. He wrote

Now I See, about the Church, and also wrote one very good novel.

In one of his books there is the story about the man who sat next to him on an airplane. Arnold was trying to read and he didn't want to be bothered talking to anyone, but this man kept asking him questions. Finally—I suppose he had developed enough from Arnold to know he liked mountain climbing—the man asked, "Do you know Arnold Lunn? He's the great mountain climber. I admire him so much." To which Arnold replied rather abruptly, "Yes, I know him. His wife is the mother of my son." The man was so shocked he didn't talk to Arnold any more during the entire journey. That was very like Arnold.

Sir Henry Lunn, his father, had this travel business and it was quite successful, but the children inherited relatively little. Arnold lived in St. Moritz. He created some of the most famous ski runs and had a great deal to do with popularizing mountain climbing and skiing. (He had this glorious son, Peter, who was a very good athlete and wrote some beautiful things and married very well. Peter was in Malta during all the dreadful bombings, and I have letters of his showing what a heroic soul he was.)

I owe to Arnold one or two voyages of enormous enjoyment. In the old days, before the Second World War, old Sir Henry ran what was called the Hellenic Cruise. Arnold would arrange for certain people to give lectures on board, and if you gave such lectures you got the trip free. So he asked me to come along and lecture. On our first voyage, we started from Venice and went down the Adriatic. It was a ship of about 14,000 tons, an English ship bought by the Yugoslav government, and we sailed down to Spoleto and other incredibly beautiful places like Ragusa (almost more beautiful than Venice), where Justinian had built temples, and further down the coast. Then we went to Greece, to Athens and on through the Aegean Sea to Constantinople, and then to the islands of Cyprus and Rhodes, to the Holy Land and back again. It took about three weeks, as I recall—probably the most enjoyable three weeks, from the human point of view, I've ever spent in my life.

There was an extremely nice set of people aboard, some enchantingly lovely: Chris Hollis, Evelyn Waugh, the Asquiths, the Lovats, the Frasers, the Cecils, Princess Mary Louise, and at the last moment the very beautiful Infanta Beatrice of Spain, granddaughter of both Queen Victoria and the Czar of Russia. Oh, there were such interesting people: judges, dons from Oxford and Cambridge—every kind of interesting person. I remember Lord Dunraven, who always carried an enormous medicine chest with him whenever he went ashore at a port. Then there was Alfred Duggan, who is supposed now to write some of the best historical novels.

Back to Arnold Lunn. As I said, I thought he got the better of Ronald Knox in some respects when they had that dispute in correspondence. It was only a part of the process whereby he was coming into the Church. Not so long after that, he finally decided that the Church was right. If he won his debate with Ronald in any way, he ended up "losing" in the sense of seeing his own position was wrong.

Another extraordinary individual was Eric Gill, the sculptor and engraver. He was a man you could never quarrel with, because he was so gentle in argument. Though he held passionate views, he never let them disturb his temper. (He wrote a very interesting autobiography, by the way.)

When he became a Catholic, he and David Jones and several others of importance formed a community in Sussex where they attempted to live in the most primitive of conditions, doing without machinery as far as possible. (Incidentally, quite nearby, but having nothing to do with this group, lived the man who did all the stations of the cross for me at Campion Hall, Frank Brangwyn. He, too, was a great artist, an astonishing creature and a very generous man. They have devoted a whole museum to him in Bruges, in Belgium. You see, though he was English, he was born in Belgium.)

Gilbert Chesterton approved of the theory of primitive community life, but he did not practice it. Eric Gill actually lived it. So does Dorothy Day, but she carries it, I think, to an extreme. Still, she's a very remarkable person. I'll tell you a very nice incident connected with her.

I knew W.H. Auden, the poet, very well. He belonged to a remarkable group of young Oxford poets, and for a short time he went Communist. Then he became, after Eliot, the number two poet of the English-speaking world. In 1938 he left England, took out American citizenship and made his home in New York. Then about five years ago he was made Professor of Poetry at Oxford, and he's just finishing out that appointment. His poetry ranks, I think, very high indeed. He's an awfully nice man. He's now become an Anglo-Catholic and is quite close to the Church. I think if Reinhold Niebuhr and his remarkable wife hadn't been so good to Auden that he became more or less tied to them, he might almost have considered the Church. At any rate, he's very near. Now, if you remember, not too long ago they were having an air raid practice where Dorothy Day lived, and she refused to pay any attention to it because she was a pacifist and felt that it would be cooperating with something military. So they ended up by fining her, and she was to be taken off to prison because she could not pay the fine, two hundred or five hundred dollars or whatever it was. There was a great crowd waiting when she came out of the court house, and somebody stepped out from the crowd and slipped the money to pay this fine into her hand. It was W.H. Auden— which was very nice, wasn't it?

But we were talking about Eric Gill. He once told me that Anthony Eden came to him one day and said, "I want you to do the sculpture for the League of Nations Building at Geneva, but you can't do anything Christian." So Gill said, "Oh, how do you expect me to do anything then?" Eden explained, "You see, there are Jews, Mohammedans and all sorts of people other than Christians in the League of Nations, and you just cannot use one particular religion. But, mind you, I don't see why you shouldn't take something from the Old Testament." Gill asked, "What about the Russians?" And Eden replied, "To hell with the Russians!" Then Gill worked out the design. I've got in my room at Farm Street the drawing which he made for it. When he died, they found written on the corner of the drawing, "This Father D'Arcy likes. Give it to him." It's a very lively, beautiful thing—quite like the famous Michelangelo of God stretching His finger out towards Adam, but I'm told Eric didn't realize that. (He must have been thinking of the Michelangelo subconsciously.) It's a beautiful drawing; but the most interesting point is that he took a line from the first chapter of the Bible, "In the image of God He created man," and then went further and wrote the beautiful inscription, "Giver of breath and bread." You see, that phrase is from Gerard Manley Hopkins. So there was put up at the great entrance to the League of Nations Hall the first lines of "The Wreck of the Deutschland," probably the first public recognition of the Jesuit poet Hopkins.

Looking back upon my life, I realize I've done nothing; but I think in a way I've sometimes perceived certain things before other people. For instance, years ago when I was a novice I came across some private diaries at one of the Jesuit houses and said, "What genius these diaries show!" So I made inquiries and was told that these were written by a Jesuit named Gerard Hopkins. Then I went up to do my philosophy, and in the library of the house of studies there was a collection by Alfred H. Miles entitled *Poets and Poetry of the XIXth Century*. There was a little paragraph about each poet, and again I saw this same Hopkins. I found about three or four poems by him and thought how wonderful they were. If only I'd had the full courage of my convictions, I'd have gone round and taken down notes from innumerable people then living who'd known Hopkins. You see, that was only 1910, and a great many of the people who had known him were then still alive. I did talk briefly with a few of them. They'd say, "Oh, yes, a most interesting man he was, a very odd little person, but a great genius and such a nice man." I once asked Father Michael Maher, the psychologist, about him, and he said, "Oh, yes, indeed, I do remember Father Hopkins. I would go to his door and look into his room, and it would be all in darkness. Then I'd hear this sepulchral voice saying, 'Who are you?' And as my eyes became accustomed to the dark, I would see Hopkins there lying on the floor. And he'd say to me, 'Oh, I'm writing poetry.' " I had a number of stories like that, you see. Alas, very few of his contemporaries seemed to have been interested in him except as an eccentric.

When I first came to the United States in 1935 and lectured on Hopkins, almost nobody'd ever heard of him. Now everybody knows more about him than I do. I remember going out to San Francisco in those days to, as I recall, Holy Name College over on the other side of the Bay. I used mischievously then to compare Hopkins with Francis Thompson, who was a kind of sacred cow at the time, you see, and I still remember a nun (a professor of English literature, I suppose) coming up to me and saying, "One line of Francis Thompson is worth all your Hopkins!"

I think Hopkins is my favorite poet, and I love his "The Windhover." I would suppose it is just about the most disputed poem in the world now. Every three or four years there is a penetrating article on what it is about. The scholars fight over this poem, and especially the Catholics. While it's called "The Windhover," it is dedicated *"To Christ our Lord,"* but I must add that *"To Christ our Lord"* was inserted years afterwards. At the time he wrote it, Hopkins himself thought that "The Windhover" was his finest poem, but then he hadn't written many of the great poems of his later years:

I caught this morning morning's minion, kingdom of
      daylight's dauphin,
Dapple-dawn-drawn Falcon, in his riding
Of the rolling level underneath him steady air, and striding
High there, how he rung upon the rein of a wimpling wing
In his ecstasy! Then off, off forth on swing,
As a skate's heel sweeps smooth on a bow-bend: the
      hurl and gliding
Rebuffed the big wind. My heart in hiding
Stirred for a bird, —the achieve of, the mastery of the thing!

Brute beauty and valour and act, oh, air, pride, plume, here
Buckle! AND the fire that breaks from thee then, a billion
Times told lovelier, more dangerous, O my chevalier!

No wonder of it: sheer plod makes plough down sillion
Shine, and blue-beak embers, ah my dear,
Fall, gall themselves, and gash gold-vermilion.

You see, the point is this: the octet, the first eight lines, are a description of this falcon as a kind of daylight's dauphin, very royal, moving, shooting up into the air. Hopkins says, "What a marvelous thing this is! My heart in hiding stirred for a bird—the achieve of, the mastery of the thing." And then comes, with an exclamation mark, "Brute beauty and valour and act! Oh, air, pride, plume, here buckle! And the fire that breaks from thee then, a billion times lovelier, more dangerous, O my chevalier. The wonder of it!" Poor Hopkins, working at the time, laboring at a desk, listening to dull theologians lecturing. It was "sheer plod makes plough down sillion shine. And blue-bleak embers, ah, my dear"—not even in a fire, you see—"fall, gall themselves, and gash, gold-vermilion."

An enormous amount turns on the word *buckle*. Everybody argues what it means. You buckle your armor when you start to go bicycling—bicycling buckling. But there's an exclamation mark. It is stated as an imperative: "Let it buckle!"

You see, certain critics, like Herbert Read and all sorts of other people, said, "Here is Hopkins, admiring beauty and the rest, and bemoaning the fact that he has given up life. It's an expression of his loathing for all that he is having to endure." To my mind, up to a point, the details aren't clear; but at one point, it's very clear to me: this is a statement of the meditation on the Kingdom of Christ. You will remember, there's the glorious Royal Prince who goes out to fight the infidels. He's all so perfect and magnificent, and then Saint Ignatius says, "Here is Christ, our King." But we're not fighting an individual. We're fighting against ourselves. It's all that hardship with yourself, self-mortification and the rest. This interpretation seems to me to work. It seems to me to make sense—especially if you put in the later dedication *"To Christ our Lord."* "I caught this morning morning's minion, kingdom of daylight's dauphin." Beautiful alliteration running through it. That's why I go to excess to bring it out in reading, because what Hopkins said was that you must even bodily produce the language and make it soar and give the physical picture.

It seems to me that Hopkins is saying that there are many problems in life and many disappointments and many things that you can't do. You have to harness yourself. But if you do, then the reward is really the greater. And he's saying that it is like our Lord Himself, who hanged upon a tree and fought and bled and buckled, in that sense, plume and pride and everything else. And how much lovelier that was! We've got faith in Him even in the chores that we do. And even black embers, when they fall, gash gold vermilion. I think that's the interpretation; but, mind you, a lot of problems remain in it.

I adore Hopkins. I find his poems so very beautiful. Forgive an Englishman for quoting "The Deutschland." You know, there were these German Franciscan sisters who had been exiled from their country. Their ship ran into a storm and was battered to pieces, and the nuns were drowned. And the great tall leader of the five nuns had been seen crying and calling out in the storm, "Oh, Christ, Christ, come quickly!" Hopkins was at St. Beuno's at the time all this occurred just off Wales. When he read about it, he was stirred beyond words. All this is about the problem of suffering in a way. It moves me deeply. It is, if you will forgive me, so very English. The end of it is like the end of a great play with a quiet and sublime ending. Notice that he puts there "Pride, rose, prince, hero of us, high-priest." And then he puts three possessives: "Our hearts' charity's hearth's fire, our thoughts' chivalry's throng's Lord." That is truly mar-velous—one of the greatest poems in the English language, I think.

Another famous writer was Max Beerbohm. I was in New York recently, and Paul Horgan, who is probably the best American Catholic writer, an awfully nice man, gave me copies of what he told me were limericks which Max Beer-bohm wrote on some of Shakespeare's plays. They may have been printed in the twenties by Gordon Craig, the son of the great Ellen Terry, in a periodical called *The Mask,* a journal devoted to the art of the theater.

The limericks went like this, as I recall:

The doings of Coriolanus
Shall not for one moment detain us.

143

Laughter and the Love of Friends

It's clear that we can't,
We won't and we shan't
Be bothered with Coriolanus.

Friend Hamlet I'm sorry to find
Unable to make up his mind;
He dillied, he dallied,
He shillied, he shallied;
In fact, he was over-refined.

There once was a Moor called Othello,
An African sort of a fellow.
When they said, "You are black,"
He cried, "Take it back:
I'm only an exquisite yellow."

There once was a king named Macbeth;
A better king never drew breath.
The faults of his life
Were all due to his wife,
Notorious Lady Macbeth.

Oxford Again

My thoughts tonight bring me back to my beloved Oxford. There are so many stories to be told of that glorious University.

Strangely enough, I would like first to say something about a Cambridge man, Bertrand Russell. As you know, he ranks as one of the most distinguished figures of our time. Most present-day books on philosophy, and mathematical philosophy especially, must have a chapter devoted to him, for he is one of the creators—indeed, *the* creator—of modern mathematical philosophy. With A.N. Whitehead he wrote that great book *Principia Mathematica,* and in many other ways he has created forms of philosophy. You may not agree with his ideas, but in many ways he's been the creative power of much of the thought in a majority of the universities of the English-speaking world and, indeed, of the German, Polish and Austrian worlds. I suppose in a way his influence has been pretty bad morally, because he's an atheist and he tried to show at one period of his life that there was nothing but the purely physical. I've been strongly against him for that reason. I've been up against him personally on two or three occasions in debates and the like.

I remember many years ago a Catholic undergraduate at Oxford, a Stonyhurst boy named Bernard Wall, who now edits periodicals and does translations for a great number of books, formed a new society. They really had got hold of top people as speakers. They had gotten Bernard Shaw, Dean Inge, G.K. Chesterton, and finally they asked Bertrand Russell and his wife, Dora. Bernard came along to me and said, "Father, I shall be so ashamed if you don't come to this meeting. You see, I was on the committee which chose Russell, and I'm feeling a bit guilty." So I said, "All right, I'll come." I might digress for a moment to say that Oxford's always been a very lucky place in the way of lectures and speakers. There's an *embarras de richesses.* You might get a truly famous name and then have only twenty people present because there would be such interesting things going on in other places. But at this particular meeting there were about five or six hundred present, I should think, and I was sitting about twenty rows down.

The chairman was a nonconformist; I seem to recollect he was a Congregationalist. At any rate, I saw him pass a note off the platform and saw it traveling down from hand to hand through the audience. You know how you get distracted: you get watching a thing like that. Finally it came to me, and I was just going to pass it on when I noticed my name on it. So I opened it and read this message: "Dear Father D'Arcy: I don't like what Russell is saying. Will you please reply to him?" Well, Russell was at the top of his reputation—and I, then as now, was a second, a backbencher, you see. So I was somewhat at a loss. Russell had gotten the reputation of being one of the ablest and sharpest minds in the world, and to tackle him on a public platform was no joke. So I said to myself, "Oh, I suppose I must. The grace of God be with me!" And when Russell had finished, the chairman got up and said, "Father D'Arcy, in the audience, will you kindly come up and make a reply?" So I went up. I am glad to say that Russell had handed himself over to me in the course of his talk. He is a curious mixture of a man. Although he has such an intensely acute mind in his own lines, he is prepared to say that he is self-contradictory and is willing to concede he has gotten no answers on certain other lines. He came out with that only a year ago, to my amazement. I hadn't, of course, realized it at the time of this debate. But he'd been passionately attacking white treatment of colored peoples and he'd gone along about ethics in his speech. Mind you, that was thirty years ago. So my point, of course, was that I didn't know why Bertrand Russell felt so strongly on this matter because, on his own assumptions, on his own philosophy, whatever happened to be his own private feelings, he didn't know whether anybody else had got private feelings; and if they did, those feelings were no concern of his; and therefore I couldn't make out why he wanted to come and tell us what our private feelings should be, because it only amounted to what we privately felt. Of course, he had no answer to that. Indeed, somebody challenged him in this same way comparatively recently, and in reply Russell wrote a letter to a well-known periodical saying, "I agree. Logically I am bound to hold that there's no answer to this question about what my private feelings are. But as a human being I simply have to say what I feel on the matter."

I can recall another occasion when he was due to speak at the Oxford Union, this time on the question of birth control. Ronald Knox was asked to answer him. Now, Ronald was one of the shyest men in the world and he hated that kind of public debate. So he wrote to the Archbishop of Birmingham asking whether he really was bound to make an answer at the Union. Word came back, "You go there and you do something." So Father Knox went, gave a short address and then left the Union Hall. The President of the Union at the time was a South African Communist. He was a Rhodes scholar, I think, and he had done an awful lot of damage just in the two or three years he had been there. In this particular case he really stacked everything against the Catholic view. A Dr. Donovan, who was a skin specialist and a member of Parliament, was the man on the side against birth control. He had never been in this terribly sophisticated Oxford Union, and he fumbled, and he wasn't clear, and he was obviously not up to the particular occasion. At any rate, he was overwhelmed by his opponents. Russell then got up and gave one of his brilliant speeches. I was there myself and got so angry that I could not resist getting up and speaking. (I was a senior member and, as one of the librarians of the Union, I had a right to speak. Also, I was sitting at the top table on this occasion.) So I got up and had my say, which was really an attack upon Russell. Now, that wouldn't seem to lend itself to too much friendship between us, would it?

Well, years afterwards, in the fifties, I was asked by the BBC to do one of those "brains trust" affairs where questions were asked you from Europe. When I was asked to do it, they said that the other members would be Bertrand Russell, Professor Alfred Ayer and some other person who was a Catholic but wasn't quite up to the others. And I said to myself, "Oh, my! I'm in for it now. Here's Russell again, this eminently first-class mind. And Ayer is the leader of the positivist philosophers of the world, with a nimble and quick mind—quick, just like lightning. And he knows all the jargon of the new views. All in all, this is going to be very difficult."

In this kind of brains trust affair you dined first at the BBC, just four or five people, and then you moved on to the room where the broadcast was going to take place. All during dinner Russell was extraordinarily nice to me. He was joking with Ayer, and they were quoting from various authors and challenging each other with quotations, you see. And as we were leaving the table before going into the broadcast room, Russell said, "Father, I owe you a deep debt of gratitude. You see, once when I was being hounded, you were the only person who would not speak against me." And then I remembered that some years before, I can't remember the time exactly, I was speaking in New York on a radio program with two or three others. (I remember one was that funny little philosopher at Columbia, the one who wrote *A Philosopher's Holiday.* I've forgotten his name now.) We were answering questions; and at the end, just before we went off the air, the chairman of the discussion said, "Now, we must end. But before we end, I'm going to ask all of you one more question. What do you think of this Bertrand Russell case?" Well, at the time I'd seen in the papers that Russell was over or coming over to the United States. He'd been appointed to a professorship at City College of New York, I believe. Somebody had written in, saying that it was almost against the Constitution that a man of this infamous character should be allowed to be a professor in an American school. And there had grown up an enormous discussion about the matter until it finally came before the courts. I think there was a good Irish judge who castigated Russell in court and, I think, denied him entry to the States. I'm not sure in my recollection now. It seems to me the charges had something to do with his passport and immigration and moral turpitude. At any rate, when the question came to me and this chairman said he wanted to know my view, I said, "I'm not going to answer this question. First of all, Bertrand Russell is an Englishman. I, too, am an Englishmen. And I don't believe in attacking one's fellow countrymen outside one's country. Then again I'm not very keen on this business of hunting down persons, pursuing them, and the rest. If you want the principles upon which a case of this sort is to be judged, I'll be glad to give them to you, but I'm not going to touch persons." By an extraordinary fluke Russell himself was listening to the program. So the chickens do come home to roost sometimes, you see. And that is why he said to me as we were leaving the BBC dinner that night, "Once when I was being hounded, you were the only person who would not speak against me."

So then we went into the broadcast room, and the first question was from Sweden: "Is there any rational argument for the existence of God?" Ayer immediately started to answer in the negative, and then I came on. Russell leaned back and after a while said, "D'Arcy's got a good point there, D'Arcy's got a very good point there." The next thing they got onto was moral evil. I was asked to begin that subject, and I gave the ordinary Catholic view. Ayer immediately said, "Completely unintelligible. That means nothing." And Russell: "Oh, no, no, that's a very good position. I rather incline to agree with what D'Arcy said on that subject. Oh, no, no, no, Ayer." So you see, it ended up as a very successful evening for me. The result was that we arranged that I should go down to dine with him later on. I spent a lovely evening with him then, and we purred together. I had the feeling that his soul could very well be saved, that there was something fundamentally nice about him despite the appalling views he'd expressed. I said to him, "You know, once upon a time you wrote books on mysticism." "I've always been interested in that subject," said he; "it's of deep interest to me." Which is a sign of hope, I think.

There are two things which made Russell, you see. The Russells are a great Whig family, and Whigs tend to hold those kinds of extreme views. But he is, I think, in a certain sense, a real gentleman. He's got many nice instincts. In talking with him I could tell how he hated all the crudities and barbarisms of so many people who quote and use him. So we were very happy together. He now is nearly ninety, but his mind has remained marvelously clear—clear as a crystal.

He's recently taken up this pacifist view again. He was put in prison in the First War as a pacifist, you know. A very mild prison, but still prison. And then in the Second World War he hated Nazism so much that he developed a belief in the just war, you see. Now he's gone back to pacifism. It's because of this nuclear question, on which he's violent. So he marched in a demonstration in the cold, bitter weather at the age of eighty-nine. There was a photograph in one of the American papers of Russell sitting down in Trafalgar Square for three hours. You saw this old man with white hair and thin face.

He has strong beliefs and feelings on these subjects relating to humanity. He's always hated, but I think never understood the reason for, authority. Therefore in his own liberalism, this Whig liberalism, he's always seen the Catholic Church as dogmatic, authoritarian, forcing opinions on people. To him, therefore, it's been a rather abhorrent thing. I think he's prepared to change his mind more now that he's come to old age. For instance, he's had a discussion with

Father Culbertson, and, please God, I think I myself have slightly disabused him of some of these mistaken opinions. Thank the Lord the authorities have been gentle with him.

He's got really an extraordinarily brilliant mind, and at the same time a wonderfully humorous one. His wit when he writes and when he speaks is astonishing. One example of his wit that I can remember was a remark he made when he was reminiscing on persons he'd known. Amongst others, he mentioned A.N. Whitehead, with whom he wrote *Principia Mathematica*. After Whitehead left Cambridge, he came over to Harvard and lived there until his death. Some people think he was the greatest philosopher of modern times, while others disagree. At any rate, he was beyond any doubt a very remarkable and a very lovely man. Now, he was the son of an Anglican clergyman, and Russell—he had a staccato way of talking—said, "You remember, of course, Whitehead. When he approached me at an early age, he had about made up his mind to be a Roman Catholic. Fortunately perhaps for the Roman Church, he fell in love and married instead."

There were several people I wish I'd known. One of them was Keynes, who, I suppose, was the greatest economist of his day. Such a brilliant man. He married one of the outstanding ballet dancers of the world—a Russian, I believe. He had a marvelous style in writing, too. He wrote a devastating book on the Versailles Treaty. And he created the whole of modern economics. There are rather violent opinions both for and against him these days. But that he bewildered and dazzled everyone by his brilliance, there can be little question.

I had marvelous tutors at Oxford. Probably the ablest mind in the whole of the last hundred years in philosophy was a man named Cook-Wilson, whom I mentioned earlier. He created a whole school of philosophers at Oxford, and they were such tremendous analytical thinkers that they couldn't utter the word *and* without pondering over it. When Russell came along to Oxford, this group despised him: they thought he was so loose in his language and inaccurate in his thought, really third-rate. They'd have a meeting and they'd tear Russell to pieces. H.W.B. Joseph, who wrote a book on logic; Pritchard, who completely destroyed Kant; the great idealist M.H.H. Joachim, and two or three others, were all in this group. I can still remember saying to Joachim, "I see that Pritchard has written an article pointing out about fifty flaws in Russell." And he replied, "I don't know why he wants to waste his time on such a second-rate thinker." So you see, I was brought up in that tradition, tutored by these men who looked down on Bertrand Russell. We did use a small book of Russell's, but really as a game, a test of how a person could think, how many inaccuracies they could find in it. (It was a little book in the *Everyman* series. I've forgotten the title of it now.) Later, when there came sweeping in through him all the new mathematical philosophies and all the things from the Viennese school, the new logics, the new criticisms, I said, "Oh, dear me, I wish I hadn't despised him so much and had kept up with him."

His is the opposite of my school, and it seems to have won the day, for the time being, through its momentum if not its logic.

Above all these men I adored Cook-Wilson. He set a mark on everybody with whom he came in contact. He was a wonderful old man. When I knew him, he was a full professor, top man. You see, there were only three or four full professors among the fifty or sixty men who would lecture in philosophy at Oxford. I'd done my scholastic work, and gaily went off to sessions with these men. And I got laid out by minds like Cook-Wilson and Joachim every time. They would say, "Oh, how interesting that view you have on *species impressa*! It is Aristotelian, of course, but the difficulty I find about that is..." and then came the devastating questions. I found that all those whom I knew as *the* great philosophical minds were realists and against the great tradition of idealism.

Somehow, I forget how I did it, I managed to become close to Cook-Wilson and used to visit him at his home. I can see him now, lying there in his garden. I think he must have had pernicious anemia. He lay in the garden in a bed, with his beautiful white beard over the bedclothes, and his wonderful piercing eyes looking at you. I think I became his favorite in a way. I would go there week after week and sit by his bedside, discussing Aristotle with him and listening and asking questions. I found he believed in freedom, believed in God, believed in immortality and in everything splendid. I was completely fascinated by him. I remember

155

the first time I went to see him. It was a steely cold, icy evening, and there in the garden as the sun set we were talking on and on. Well, when I finally started to get out of my seat, I was almost frozen and I could hardly get up. I was utterly fascinated by this marvelous old man talking, and his influence on me was gigantic. In a certain sense, it was what made me. I was a scholastic at the time; and his training made me, I think, in the sense of tempering my mental equipment.

But he had the faults of his genius. He was always sending in to the Admiralty some marvelous inventions about blowing up submarines or something of the sort. He was a wonderful all-around man, a philosopher, a mathematician, a scientist. Once he got hold of a subject, he couldn't leave it alone; he'd tear it and tear it and tear it, until he got to the bottom of it.

I once heard a wonderful story about him in this regard. There used to be a thing called the Philological Society in Oxford. All the great classical scholars of the day belonged to it. Cook-Wilson and Gilbert Murray and other great scholars who loved comparing religions and were always finding that the Christian religion was very like the *mithra* worship. Well, this particular time, one of them came out with the view that all Homer was patchwork; and he said that one of the things that proved it was that when you had similes such as "like the lion that seizes its prey," the similes didn't seem to have very much to do with the story. On the strength of that, these great scholars said that the simile was an interpolation, didn't belong in the original text, and showed patchwork.

The great Cook-Wilson listened to this theory but was unconvinced. He was always for what I call the orthodox view. So he labeled this view as "modern nonsense" and came home from the meeting determined to show that the theory wasn't true. He therefore wrote Sir Walter Raleigh— the top professor of English Literature at the time, a great scholar in his way and author of some lovely things—and asked him to list for him the poets who most use simile and metaphor. "You know," he told me, "I got a contemptuous letter back from Sir Walter Raleigh saying, 'All poets use simile and metaphor. I don't know what you're concerned about, but I suggest the following names.' Well, when I proceeded to got through all the English poets, I found the people he suggested were the ones who used simile and metaphor the least!" When he'd done that, he read a paper to the Philological Society showing that this simile approach was a completely wrong test and that every respectable poet did the same thing as Homer did. Well, he started reading his paper at this meeting. Arthur Evans, of Crete and Cnossus fame, apparently came in a few minutes late. He listened for a time and then got up and said, "Mr. Chairman, may I ask a question? What's this all about?" Another hour and a half passed, and Arthur got up again: "Here, what is this all about?" Finally, he just walked out. The talk had started about eight o'clock. By half past eleven nearly everybody had crept out, but Cook-Wilson went on and on and on

proving his point. By twelve o'clock really everybody had
left and only the President and the Secretary were there. So
the President said, "Professor, don't you think we'd better
stop?" "Stop? I've hardly reached the most important part!"
In the end, he stopped only on the condition that he would
continue the paper at the next meeting—which ruined the
Philological Society, because they did not dare meet for fear
he would continue! Yet he was a great man, one of the truly
interesting and great people of the time.

I have mentioned the name of Gilbert Murray. He was a
tremendous scholar. There was a considerable controversy
about whether be became a Catholic on his deathbed, you
know. The London *Tablet* had quite a bit about it. I was
pulled into the matter myself. This was only a year or two
ago, you see, and I had just got back from the United States,
from Georgetown, when he died. Gilbert was a great humanist—a kind of sacred cow to the humanists, enormously
admired especially in his old age. He had married Mary Murray of the Earl of Carlisle house, a very strong woman. They
had a number of children and brought them up quite
strangely. They were vegetarians and never touched a drink.
Most of the children were somewhat odd because they had
this unusual upbringing.

One of them became a Catholic. That was Rosalind, a
brilliant woman (she's still alive) who wrote two or three
books—one, I think, being *The Good Pagan's Failure*. She
married Arnold Toynbee but divorced him during the First
World War. That was terribly sad in every way. Toynbee at

the end of his first volumes—he was almost at the point of becoming a Catholic—practically said that Christianity was a solution to all history. Then came the war and this divorce. That really destroyed him, I think, because he's written nonsense ever since, almost hysterical nonsense. His last volumes were not equal to the first at all. He tutored me at Oxford, you know. He was an awfully nice man.

Oxford again. I am reminded of a story connected with mighty Balliol. During the Second World War (I think it must have been 1941), I was on my way to the United States, and we had to fly from Bristol. We were to fly to Lisbon first, on a Dutch plane, and as we were walking out to the plane a man came up to me and said, "You're Father D'Arcy, aren't you?" I answered, "Yes." And he said, "My name is MacIntosh. I'm going over to the States for the government on economic matters. I write ballads, and Chesterton and Belloc have been great friends of mine. In fact, we produced books together. Please sit next to me so we can talk." So we sat together, and he proved to be an extraordinary character, a most remarkable man. I liked him very much. He had a phenomenal memory: anything he heard he remembered. I've got in my pocketbook poems which he wrote out ten or twelve thousand feet up over the Atlantic, poems which he remembered word for word but which I knew nothing of—lovely medieval ballads. He also wrote out for me something I ought to have known, the famous "Ballad to Our Lady of Czestochowa" by Belloc. I think I've still got that in my pocketbook. He could memorize things in

English, French, German, Spanish and Russian, and he could just go on and on. Altogether an astonishing person.

When we landed at Lisbon, we were told we would have to wait since the old clipper that was to take us to New York wasn't going for a day or two because of weather. I was stranded because I had no place to live and no money. And this MacIntosh said, "Oh! Do come and be my guest at the hotel in Estoril." So I went. After about four days we received word we could start out, and on a gray, cold, damp, miserable morning we arrived at the terminal in Lisbon from Estoril. Everybody was irritable and miserable as we got into the car to take us out to the airport. While we were sitting in the car, a fussy man came up to us and asked, "Have you got my bag? Are you sure you haven't got my bag?" We said, "No, we haven't got your bag." As he went away, I turned to MacIntosh and asked, "Who do you think that is?" He said, "I don't know. Obviously a greengrocer." I said, "No, I'm sure you're wrong. I think he's a Balliol man." "A Balliol man?" "Yes, I think with that accent he's a Balliol man."

Then we got on the plane, and I heard this strange man talking in what I thought was an extremely cultured and brilliant manner. He was dressed very carelessly and looked like nothing on earth. I can still remember some image he was using about how chickens come home to roost. His phrasing was beautiful, and I said to myself, "That's a clever man." Well, we arrived at the Azores and had another three days' wait there, what with winds and storms and fogs. While we were waiting at the Pan-American Club, the call boy suddenly came around shouting, "Professor Tawney, Professor Tawney," and up came our fussy little man. And I said, "I was right." It was R.H. Tawney, probably the greatest Balliol man of his time. Indeed, many Oxford men regard him as the outstanding man produced by Oxford in the last generation.

Tawney wrote a book called *The Acquisitive Society,* another called *Religion and the Rise of Capitalism,* and one or two others. He was a great Christian, a Catholic, and a man who inspired enormous respect. He took up what was called the Educational Workers Establishment, a series of clubs and societies and colleges in cities to help give the workingman an education. He was the leading person in that movement and, in fact, gave his life to it. At the same time, he was regarded as one of the greatest men on social economics. He had this great slant to give more Christian values to it. And here he was, going out to Washington during the war to give advice on economic matters. Apparently his traveling bag contained some very valuable things that he oughtn't to have lost, and that's why he was in such a state of worry. When I discovered this, I went up to him and we got friendly and I said, "I'm afraid we were a bit stiff." And he replied, "Yes, you behaved very badly to me."

Only about a week ago Winston Churchill had a birthday, and *The New York Times,* I think it was, mentioned that it was also the birthday of R.H. Tawney. It brought back memories to me. I can still remember as an undergraduate talking with a master of Balliol, who recounted what an absent-minded genius Tawney was: how when he got home once, tired and exhausted and wanting a bath, he undressed and, instead of getting into the tub, threw all his clothes in; and again, how another habit of his was to light a pipe during his lectures and stick it into his pocket all hot and alight, while everybody watched to see if the pocket would burst into flame. He is a very great man, one of the greatest men living, I think. And I'm proud that I recognized the Balliol accent.

Heroic Figures

I have already confessed to being something of a hero worshipper, and there are a small number of figures I adore in English history. One is Sir William Longsword, Earl of Salisbury, who was the great knight at the time of Henry III and went to Palestine and died for the cross out there. His effigy is in Salisbury Cathedral. Then I adore Edward, the Black Prince. But above all others, my beloved St. Thomas More, the Duke of Wellington and, lastly, Winston Churchill. I think these three figures are gigantic.

The Duke of Wellington is to my mind one of the really great figures of history. Everything he said had a tang to it— like Samuel Johnson, like Belloc: every sentence they uttered had a certain quality which is so personal to them. Wellington had that. When you read the great diaries of the time, those of Greville and various other people, you see that as soon as Wellington arrives on the scene, or comes for the weekend, everyone else ceases to exist. His remarks are so defined and clear. Let me give you some examples as I recall them.

Wellington was once walking down Piccadilly when a man came up and greeted him, "Mr. Smith, I believe."

Wellington looked at him and said, "Sir. If you believe that, you'll believe anything."

Did you know that a nephew of his became a Passionist priest? (The young man was a Pakenham. You see, the Duke of Wellington married into the Pakenham family; his wife was a Pakenham.) The nephew was, from what I've seen of portraits of him, a very tall, ascetic, handsome man. When the Duke heard that he'd become a convert and wanted to be a Passionist, an Irish Passionist at that, he is supposed to have said, "My boy, if you're going to do that, make sure you do it well." So typical of the Duke, I think.

Again, I remember reading a marvelous Wellington story in *The London Times* years and years ago. The Duke had won one of his memorable victories in Spain and had to move on to a camp about twenty miles away, leaving the wounded behind. When he pitched his camp he said to himself, "I'm sure they won't be looking after the wounded." So he rode all the way back and, sure enough, found the wounded not properly tended. He then gave very strict orders about tending the wounded and returned to his camp. After a while he thought, "Now they'll be sure to think I will never get back again." So back he went to make certain that they were paying attention to his orders and to the wounded. Any man who does that is to my mind first rate, first quality. There were in him all sorts of splendid characteristics of that type. I can think of two delightful incidents to illustrate.

Wellington was coming up from the country to Apsley House. It was located just there at the edge of Hyde Park and had been given to him by the nation. (Still, he had to put up iron gates around the property when people turned against him during the socialist, liberal movement. Very few realize that he was the man who gave the Catholics emancipation.) Well, he was coming up from the country in his carriage when he met a small boy on the way near Hyde Park. When he saw the boy was crying, he had his carriage stopped and asked, "My boy, what's the matter?" And the boy said, "I've got a golden toad that I adore. But I'm going to Eton, and they won't allow me to bring my toad with me. When I leave, it will die because it needs all these special kinds of herbs to live." And the Duke said, "All right, my boy. I'll look after it." So he took the toad back to Apsley House and used to send his servants out every day to Hyde Park to pick the particular herbs needed to keep this toad alive.

Now the other incident. I think it is one of the loveliest stories told about Wellington. He had hired this contractor to build his house. (The nation was very generous in those days to its heroes, as is America too. None of that nasty niggardly way which has grown on people now.) Let's call this contractor Clifton, since I can't remember his actual name. So one day Wellington said, "Clifton, you've been very good to me. I'd like to do something for you. What can I do? Tell me now." And the man said, "Sir, there's nothing you can do for *me*. But, you know, I have a daughter, a little girl, and she's at school in Kensington. And, sir, it's a fashionable school; and since I'm nobody, my little girl is rather looked down upon. If you could just say a word for her, sir, I would be so grateful." "Good," said the Duke. So he went back to Apsley House, ordered out his great barouche with his postillions and drove out to a place where he could pick up some flowers. Then he went on to this school in Kensington and, upon his arrival, identified himself to the headmistress as the Duke of Wellington. Of course, he was the greatest figure in the world at this time. So the whole of the school came out, absolutely flustered beyond words. The students had been assembled straightaway and marched in before this splendid figure. Then he boomed out, "Miss Clifton, Miss Mary Clifton! Where is she?" And this rather shrinking, nice little child came forward. So he handed her this bouquet of flowers and he kissed her and said, "Mary, your father and I are great friends. What they do to you here at this school they do to me. If they treat you well, they treat me well; if they treat you badly, they treat me badly. I hope they'll be *good* to you. God bless you, my child." And out he went to his carriage and drove off.

There was a story about a famous courtesan who saw her past as a means of establishing herself in great riches by blackmail. She wrote around to a lot of prominent people—including the Duke of Wellington, who had never had anything to do with her—saying, "I'm going to write my reminiscences. If you will send me £ 1,000 (or £ 5,000 or £ 10,000), I will leave your name out." Practically all of them yielded, except the Duke of Wellington, who wrote, "Publish and be damned." It was so magnificent.

I am reminded of the Duke of Windsor. He came up to Oxford as the Prince of Wales the very year I did. I once heard a story against him, but it's such a good story I think he'd forgive me for telling it. I used to know a man named Richard Tobin. He came from California and he'd been Ambassador in Holland. He married a connection of the Vanderbilts, and they had a lovely place in Long Island. One day he invited me to lunch. Well, the door was opened by a magnificent-looking butler to whom, when he spoke, I said, "You sound as if you were English." He said, "Oh, I am English, sir." After lunch as we were moving round the garden, I said to Mr. Tobin, "You've got a very fine-looking butler." And he said, "Oh, he's a most remarkable man. He was magnificent in the war. He has all sorts of decorations. And," he continued, "I'll tell you something about him. One evening I was having the Duke and Duchess of Windsor to dine with me, so I turned to him and said, 'John, I'm having the Duke and Duchess of Windsor to dine tonight. If you like, you can wear your decorations.' He paused, looked me in the face and said, 'Sir, I should prefer not to wear my decorations if you do not mind. Indeed, if you do not mind, sir, could you forgive me for not serving tonight? I do not believe in a king who deserts his people.' " Now, that was such a magnificent statement: all the kind of old conception of Christian kingship: like a shepherd of his flock, you know, or a colonel with his regiment—only to a much higher degree, like a priest leaving his parish when his people are suffering. I think the whole of the history of Christendom is in that statement, even though it wasn't quite fair to the Duke.

Well, now back to the Duke of Windsor himself. I think he has great intelligence and also great generosity of spirit. Moreover, he is a religious man in his way. The detective who accompanied him on his first travels abroad happened to be a very good Catholic who had boys in one of our schools and he told me that he would sometimes drop in late at night and find the young Prince of Wales on his knees, praying. He did some wild things as a young man, I know: he used to get bored too quickly and sometimes did things that were a little foolish. But he always had that amazing sense of what was due to persons, and was ready to sacrifice himself for them. Physically also he was a man without fear. During the First World War, you know, he was at the front, and they were always a little frightened that he would slip away and get into some dangerous position, so they kept a careful eye on him.

As you can see, I've always had a high regard for the Prince of Wales (as I always think of him) and am sorry it was not my good fortune to have known him personally.

One of the really great regrets of my life is that I didn't insist on certain of my friends arranging that I meet and get to know Winston Churchill. Katherine Asquith and some other friends of his were intimate friends of mine and they were always saying to me, "We know you admire Winston

so much. We must have the two of you together for dinner."
But, alas, it never came off, and I've regretted it all my life.
All during that period of the thirties I swore by Winston
Churchill. He was out, you see, but I felt he was *the* man. I
had enormous admiration for him.

I can still remember something that happened, I suppose
it was about 1940, or possibly before that. At any rate, I was
making a stay at Georgetown at the time, and Father Ed-
mund Walsh met me in the hall just outside of his room. He
had a book in his hand and he said, "It's all here: the whole
of the future, everything that's going to happen. If people
would only listen to this!" And the volume contained the
speeches of Churchill, you see, in the thirties. They showed
what a prophetic power he had.

Churchill's friends have always loved him. He never lost
that happy touch of friendship. Even when he was at his
highest, he was a tremendously loyal and devoted friend—
tremendously human. That's one of the reasons I like him so
much. A man may be a genius but at the same time de-
testable—for example, a man like Lloyd George—but
Churchill is a genius *and* honorable *and* loved.

In speaking about Churchill—well, where shall I begin?
I knew his sister-in-law very well. You see, Winston
Churchill had a younger brother, Major John Churchill.
(They were the grandchildren of the Duke of Marlborough.
Their father was Lord Randolph Churchill, who married an
American, and that's why Churchill has American blood in
him.) Major John Churchill married Lady Gwendolyn Ber-

tie. She was of a family which had become Catholic converts, the Earls of Abingdon. Lady Gwendolyn (she was always called Goonie by her friends) was a lovely and charming person, a very good person, and a Catholic, but she had only the vaguest knowledge of her religion.

Well, she became a great friend of mine, partly because she was very close to the Asquiths. Her daughter very nearly married Katherine Asquith's son, now the Earl of Oxford, but the match just never worked out. The girl went up to Oxford and for a while sat under that extraordinary genius, Isaiah Berlin. Finally, in recent years she married Anthony Eden and has been a very good wife to him in his illnesses and other trials. I was told a charming story about her recently. As a result of her upbringing, I don't think she ever knew much about her religion. But she was with her husband on some weekend, and they went to the village church. And Mr. Butler, who's the second-in-command of the British government, started singing away some hymn. He noticed Mrs. Eden wasn't singing and turned to her and said, "Come on, come on, why don't you sing?" And she replied, "I don't sing here. I'm a Catholic."

Lady Gwendolyn knew of my admiration for Winston Churchill and from time to time she would talk to me about him. I can recall telling her, when I was building Campion Hall, that I wanted to have a chapel which I hoped the old Duke of Marlborough, a staunch convert, might be willing to pay for. (You see, Blenheim Palace was only some few miles out of Oxford.) And Goonie said to me, "Oh, I think that's a great idea. I believe Winston would back that." My response was, "I think it will work out, but not through Winston, though I'd be glad of his help." (It didn't work out, but not through any fault of Churchill's.) Then Goonie said to me, "You know, I wouldn't be a bit surprised if Winston someday becomes a Catholic. When he's finished with politics, his mind will move in that direction." That apparently has not happened. But I am satisfied myself that he is fundamentally a religious man.

As you know, the Duke of Marlborough had become a convert when he married Consuela Vanderbilt and then there came all the trouble, the famous Marlborough annulment case. But he became a very firm and fixed Catholic and he had some dreadful times as a consequence. Once he went to confession to Father Roy Steuart and at the end of confession he said, "Father, what do I do with this?" And he showed Father Steuart a host. He said, "This kind of thing happens to me. Hateful and horrible things! Someone sent me this in the mail saying it was a consecrated host." Isn't that horrible? It only shows the hatred of God, you see. When it comes out, a devilish kind of spirit takes over. One of the best proofs of the divinity of Christ, actually.

Well, when the Duke of Marlborough died, there was a Requiem for him at Farm Street and then the body was taken by train to Blenheim. (That is the place given the original Duke by Queen Anne after his great military victories. All that the Dukes of Marlborough have to do to keep Blenheim is present a flag every year to their monarch.) So the body, as I said, was taken there to be buried. I suppose Goonie Churchill was in the same carriage with the new Duke and Winston Churchill. At any rate, she said the new Duke, who was a huge man, about six feet seven or so, but not an intellectual type, turned to Winston and commented, "Well, it was all rather hocus-pocus, that service we've just been attending." And she said Winston leaned across the carriage and said to the Duke, "You nitwit! That was a most beautiful ceremony. The truth is, you don't understand it. Now I'll explain it to you." And with that he picked out of his pocket one of those little Requiem Mass leaflets that are presented to everybody at Catholic funerals, and right then and there in the carriage proceeded to explain it to the Duke.

Now, another instance to show Churchill's mind on religion. When I got back from America about 1943 or so, I learned that Gwendolyn Churchill had just died and was to be buried at a place called Begbroke, about six miles outside of Oxford. Her family, the Abingdons, had a vault there, and the Servite Fathers keep a church and novitiate nearby. So I got into my little car and drove out there. To my astonishment, as we got near the church I found children holding flags lining the way, and policemen all about the place. Soon I saw my beloved Mrs. Asquith and Lady Helen Asquith and asked them what was going on. They said, "Winston is coming to the funeral. So that's why all this stir." Surely enough, Churchill arrived, and Katherine Asquith told me later that he was very moved by the funeral service.

The next day I met the Servite Prior of that church, Father Gerald McCarthy, on the street in Oxford and said to him, "That was very interesting yesterday, wasn't it?" And he said, "Indeed it was! And I'll tell you something you may not know. Before the Prime Minister arrived, Lady Abingdon came up to me and said, 'Father, at the graveside could you have some of the service said in English? My son-in-law is such a religious man and he'd love to be able to join in, but I expect his Latin is now a bit rusty.' A bit later John Churchill came up and said, 'My brother is quite religious-minded. Could you say some of the prayers in English at the graveside so he may join in?' So of course I did as they requested. And when it was over, the Prime Minister himself came over to me to thank me for it. So I said to him, 'Sir, this is a great occasion for us, to have you here. We are all praying for you and for our cause.' And he said, 'Thank you. We need your prayers very much. Our cause is just. It is a great and just cause. I know it, I know it. And God is on our side. But, you know, we are not out of the woods yet. We are not out of the woods yet.' Then I said, 'But you are right, sir: God is with us.' And Churchill said, 'That is so true. I've never felt the truth of that so much as in the last three weeks. I have felt the Holy Spirit was with me these days.' " Now, a man who is not religious doesn't talk that language. People sometimes say that Winston Churchill hasn't any interest in religion, but these little incidents show that's obviously quite wrong. I'm so glad, too, because I regard him as one of the greatest men living—indeed, one of the great men of history—and I always like to see those men have a sense of God and religion.

As you know, Churchill wrote the story of his early life and in it told how, after he left Harrow, he read a book by a very famous man which bitterly attacked God and religion on the ground of all the pain and suffering in the world; and how that book changed him and turned him into an agnostic or an atheist (I've forgotten which now). Then he went on to say that this had been during his youth, and that experience had taught him a wisdom far different from that. I forget just how he expressed it, but he meant that he was different now in his beliefs from what he had been as a young man. Well, a number of years ago I wrote a book called *The Nature of Belief*. In it I was very strong for the fact that experience can affect the mind and that a real person sees certain things in a different light as he moves through life—in short, as he gains wisdom from experience. And I quoted this passage from Churchill's book as showing him to be a man to whom actual experience, rather than mere reading or anything else, had brought wisdom. To my great surprise one day Maurice Baring told me that he had sent a copy of my book to Churchill, whom he knew very well indeed. And Maurice said he had marked the passage where I referred to Churchill. I've always been pleased about that. It rather created an invisible relationship between us.

Winston Churchill is also a magnanimous man. I'll give an instance to show this in his relations with Stanley Baldwin. You see, as Prime Minister, Baldwin had kept him out, wouldn't have him in the government at all. So during that period, poor Churchill was out of everything altogether, just watching the world fall to pieces and feeling that nothing at all was being done. Then he came on during the war finally, and became Prime Minister. At any rate, Baldwin came up to London during the war, and Churchill heard about it. Immediately he invited the old man to lunch and not only gave him an excellent meal but also showed him all that was happening in the conduct of the war, the preparations, the secret things, and everything else. That was an act, you see, of generosity.

Which reminds me of a story told me by a secretary of Churchill's—one of the most marvelous stories of the Second War. It was in those dark months just before the invasion of Africa (which was called "Torch") and there were top secret documents which only the very highest officials could see. Well, there was this officer in Whitehall round about a quarter of six in the evening. (I've forgotten his name but I'll call him Major Stanley.) He was due to get off at six and was preparing to leave when suddenly a messenger knocked at the door, came in, and plunked down a document on his desk. He opened the outside envelope and saw "Top Secret Document." Well, he was tempted, and it is easy to understand the temptation because at that hour of the day he could very well rationalize that little could be done. So he said to himself, "Oh, well, I'll put this into my satchel, take it home, and pass it on tomorrow." Then he left his office and went down into Whitehall—into the city's dark, blacked-out streets. Sitting here now, you have no conception of the wartime blackout in a country like England—rainy, wet, bleak, eerie. The streets were pitch black, and Stanley stood there under a bus sign waiting for the #1 Bus in the mud and the wet and the dark. Finally he got his bus, got home, and opened his satchel just to have a glance at the paper. But there was no top secret document in it! You can imagine his feelings: his own career, that of the Prime Minister, the danger to his country...

Well, next morning, a certain Miss Brown, a charwoman, was walking down Whitehall and, in the mud, she noticed a largish piece of paper. So she bent down, picked it up, took one glance at it and immediately rushed straight across to Scotland Yard and handed it in. She said to the officer at the desk, "Here—this isn't for the likes of me." He looked at it, saw right off it was a top secret document and had it taken straight across to Whitehall. Churchill heard immediately, made inquiries as to what had happened, then said, "Cashier Major Stanley. Then, when you've cashiered him, restore him to his rank and office again. He made a mistake, but he's a fine officer and will have learned his lesson." That again shows the greatness of the man. "Now," he said, "we must do everything for Miss Brown. She must receive the highest honors of the land." So he undertook to find out what honors he could give her. Now, the only honors for a person like that lay in what is called the Order of the British Empire: Commander, Officer or Member of the British Empire. Those are the three ranks, you see. So he recommended Miss Brown for Commander of the British Empire. At the end of a year, he found that there was such a resistance (it's impossible for a person other than a colonel or a general or a member of the cabinet to be made a Commander) that he recommended her as an Officer of the British Empire. But he was told that was impossible, so he proposed Miss Brown as a Member of the British Empire. Well, that was the situation at the end of the war.

This man who told me the story (in 1949 or 1950, I suppose) said that, only a week before, he had driven with Churchill to Harrow, his old school, where he goes every year to sing the famous Harrow songs, extremely moving, wonderfully intoxicating songs. And my friend told me that on the way up he said to Churchill, "Oh, tell me, sir, whatever has happened to Miss Brown?" The reply was, "I'll tell you what has happened to Miss Brown. I'm still *struggling* to get the honors that are due her!"

To me Winston Churchill is the greatest man of his generation; certainly I do not see anyone who is bigger. I have such hopes that your President Kennedy may in a way be like him. I think he has modeled himself to a degree on Churchill who is like one of those *Profiles in Courage* that Kennedy wrote when he was sick. The President likes a man of that type and quotes him frequently. Few people have the gift of language that Winston Churchill has and if I, an Englishman, may say so, I don't think that Kennedy quite meets him there. As who does? For instance, Ramsay Mac-Donald, the Labor Prime Minister, was a gifted man but a man who just talked and talked. Churchill said of him, "That boneless wonder! The maximum of words for the minimum of meaning." He's full of those phrases. I think it was Katherine Asquith who told me that once when they were playing chess at her home, Churchill strolled across, looked at the board and said, "Move that Baldwin," meaning the pawn. Full of life, isn't he? He is an astonishingly gifted man in his description of people. He can always capture some phrase which is quite intoxicating. Indeed, almost everything he says is magnificent.

Once—I know a man who actually heard the exchange—Churchill was speaking in the House of Commons and apparently irritated enormously a man named Paling on the opposite side, the Labor side. Finally Paling got so angry at something Churchill said that he bounced to his feet and shouted, "You—you dirty dog! How dare you say that to me? How dare you do that to me?" And Churchill, with scarcely a pause, said, "If you will come outside the House, I'll show you what a dirty dog does to a paling!"

A Group of Eccentrics

Dame Edith Sitwell is a great friend of mine. When I was over in America about four years ago she sent me word asking, "Father, what should I do? I want so much to become a Catholic." I wrote back and arranged for Father Philip Caraman to instruct her, and she came into the Church. She looks much like a medieval nun. She has this wonderful, amazingly pale face, which has been sculptured, of course, and she wears great jewels on her fingers. And she is quite a remarkable person: poet, critic and novelist. Among her books is an amusing one called *English Eccentrics*. It interested me especially because I seem to have known so many individuals who might qualify as eccentrics. Of course, Dame Edith really did not have to go outside her own family to find an eccentric. Her own father was quite unusual himself, as Osbert Sitwell shows in his reminiscences. They're too good for words, I think. First of all, they're a classic; they're among the finest of modern writings. But beyond that, his sense of humor is so very good. Some people have said he shouldn't have written about his father as he did. I must own I don't agree. The father was certainly an incredibly selfish and really horrible man, and

Osbert did not hide this fact but, instead, turned him into a character you rather enjoyed.

I love these eccentric people in a way. I'm reminded again of the story about the father of my friend, the present Earl of Wicklow. In the days before World War II, he lived on this enormous estate he had down in Wicklow—thousands of acres of land and a gigantic house of about eighty or a hundred rooms. Well, he was one of the old Irish landlords and he'd grown more crotchety and queer with the years. For example, while he kept some two hundred gardeners, he had only one house servant. When he wanted to light his cigar, he would just pull a precious book off the shelf and tear a page out of it. He disapproved terribly of his son, Billy Wicklow, becoming a Catholic. Well, about 1939 Billy turned up at his father's place and spent several days quite unsuccessfully trying to impress upon the old man the great danger that Hitler posed to world peace. Finally, one evening he found his father in the library poring over an atlas; and the old man said to Billy, "Hmph. What's this place—Czechoslovakia—you've been talking about? I can't even find it in my atlas." So Billy said, "But, Father, that atlas of yours is about a hundred years old. Czechoslovakia wouldn't be carried in it." At which his father slammed the book closed and stood up, saying, "Not even in the atlas, eh? Well, that turns the whole thing into a bloody farce!" I think that recreates the whole atmosphere of a period.

Then there was a man who was supposed to be one of the two most evil men of the times—Montague Summers.

(The other was Alistair Crowley, who was said to go in for black magic.) I knew Summers because he settled in Oxford. As an Oxford man myself, I always felt he probably was a Cambridge man, being what he was! It was said that Cambridge had banned him so that he couldn't live there. At any rate, he did live in Oxford in an apartment just next door to the Dominican Priory. He used to like to go to the Dominican liturgical services, to the horror of the community. The charming Prior (who was Jesuit-educated, incidentally) was always afraid that Summers might come up to Communion, and one day he did come up to the altar rail at Communion time. So the Prior waited for him afterward and spoke to him about it. Summers never came back to the Priory. I don't quite know what his position was religiously. He had been, I think, a deacon or subdeacon in the Anglican Church. There was a story, apparently based to some extent on fact, that he tried to become a Catholic and even a priest. But, according to the story, the Church was saved because the Catholic bishop of the diocese where Summers was attempting to make entry happened one day to sit in the same railway carriage with an Anglican bishop who told him the facts about Summers, and that ended his chances of a career as a Catholic priest. He did usually wear ecclesiastical garb, and he was a fat, greasy man. He was supposed to be something of an authority on seventeenth-century plays and on the incubus and succubus and all sorts of medieval monstrosities. As I have said, he was held by some to be a very wicked man. I myself think he was probably a harmless ass.

Well, when he settled down in Oxford, he used to have with him a very pasty-faced boy and a mongrel dog. Whenever he went out for walks, he always had either the pasty-faced boy or the dog with him, but never both of them. They were never seen together. The legend grew up among the undergraduates that they were identical, this dog and this pasty-faced boy. At any rate, some of the undergraduates at Balliol tried to scheme one day to get more information on Summers. They invited the boy to come to lunch at Balliol, about the fourth staircase up. And they offered him a glass of sherry before they started to eat. He took the sherry and started to drink it, when suddenly he went into a trance and got quite fixed. (Somebody told me this who was there, but whether he was making some of it up, I don't know.) He stood there transfixed for a moment or two, turned round, walked out of the room, descended all those four staircases holding this glass of sherry in his hand, went out by the great doors of Balliol, across St. Giles (a very wide, busy thoroughfare, with traffic running through it), and back to the Montague Summers apartment. And that's quite a tale, I think.

Frederick Rolfe, "Baron Corvo," was another extraordinary figure of that period, and some of his writings are still fashionable. He was accustomed to use the library we had at Farm Street in his day. You see, Farm Street in London used to have a large library, a very good library, but it was mainly bombed out in the Second War. (Father Caraman put that right and has restored everything.)

Frederick Rolfe was really a mysterious person. I don't think people know very much about him or his origins, but he appears as a rather fantastic figure who wrote a number of books, had the most beautiful handwriting, and longed to be a priest. At one stage, when he was dreadfully impoverished, he went to Wales and arrived at our church, St. Winefred of the Well at St. Asaph. (There was a well there where miracles had been worked for centuries. Hopkins describes it in the play *St. Winefred's Well.*) The priest at the time, a Father Beauclark, thinking it would help Rolfe, got him to do some painting for the church just to keep him going. For that work this man then sent a bill for something unbelievable, like fifty thousand pounds. There was a royal row over this bill, and he came to regard Father Beauclark as his mortal enemy. You see, he had this dreadful persecution mania. He was constantly being taken up by people, but always ended up by turning against them.

He wrote some interesting books and became a fantastic figure. His novel *Hadrian the Seventh* is in a way a classic. All his enemies are brought into the book, quite ill-disguised. He has an Englishman become Pope (that's obviously himself), and he makes delightful attacks upon everybody he hates. One of the first things the Pope does when he's elected is to have a Requiem for Queen Victoria. It was very comic in a way, though he didn't realize it. When the Jesuit General (Rolfe couldn't abide the Jesuits, you see) comes in to see the Pope, in a red-faced and truculent manner, with his snuff box, the Pope says peremptorily, "Put that snuff box away!" It is a most interesting book. Then there are two volumes about a charming Italian child who tells the most wicked stories about how the simple Franciscans were deceived by the Jesuits. You know those tales, but they are rather amusing if read in the right light. And he wrote quite a number of other books. They have a rarity value now. He finally ended up going to Venice and there he wrote his last book, *The Desire and Pursuit of the Whole*. He got lonelier and lonelier, and suffered more and more from this persecution complex. There is a great fear that he may have committed suicide.

Another unusual person was a woman who was known all over London for her most extraordinary hats, heavily powdered face, strangely piercing eyes, and uninhibited remarks. I can see her now, walking down Bond Street and everyone staring at her. I cannot recall her name, but she was related to some Duke and figured in many of the novels of the period—D.H. Lawrence, Aldous Huxley and the rest. She was painted by Augustus John (rather cruelly, as I thought). The story I like most about her relates to the time her husband was fighting for his seat in the House of Commons, and she insisted upon helping him. Now, her husband thought no end of himself and his family, which was really nothing compared to her family. And once when he'd finished a political talk, she got on to the platform and said, "Oh, my darling people, I love you so. After all, I married into you." She was a fantastic woman and, as I say, she figured in many of the novels of the period.

When I speak of unusual personalities, I can never leave out a marvelous cousin of mine. I'd like to tell you something about him, though I'm afraid I can't at this moment create an image of him which would be as good as I should like. In a certain way he's a mystery man. About 1932, I should think, I happened to be at a gathering in Oxford when this smallish man, who talked with a touch of an Irish brogue and had one of those old, aristocratic Irish faces, introduced himself to me as being a connection of mine. He said his name was Paddy Shannon and that he was some sort of a cousin. I don't know to this day exactly how he's related to me, but over the years I've grown to believe most things he says. At the time we met, he told me he was working on the history of the D'Arcy family, and that did excite me greatly. I was deeply interested in the subject but, frankly, knew very little about the D'Arcys except for chance remarks made by my father. And Paddy told me more about them than I'd been able to find out from all other sources put together.

I became very intimate with Paddy, going for walks with him every day at Oxford and so on. He was very flush of money in those days and used to entertain royally for the undergraduates. Apparently he had been for a time in India in the army, and in the Dragoon Guards, I think, and said he'd known the Prince of Wales just at the beginning of World War I. (I'm giving you his own story as he told it to me.) He got very badly wounded in that war and had been something of an invalid every since. I discovered later that he was a

185

"bleeder" and that the condition got worse and worse, so that now he's apt to be in grave danger if he's cut or bruised or bleeds for any reason. Well, as I say, he seemed enormously rich in the early days, and it was very difficult to stop him doing things for you. If you passed a shop and he saw you look with interest at a thing in the window, he'd say, "Would you like that, Father?" And right away he'd buy it for you.

In those days he would plunge, promising things to people and getting himself into awkward situations. He'd say, "Oh, I'll see to that," or "Oh, you're in debt? Don't worry about it. I'll take care of it." As a result of such remarks, I think that on occasion he felt he had to pay certain debts of other people and after a time he found himself rather short of money. Even so, he was continually pressing things on one. He had the most wonderful collection of rare items, really extraordinary treasures. For instance, once when Ronald Knox went to lunch with him in his place in Scotland, he served a complete luncheon on D'Arcy silver. And he's got all sorts of eighteenth-century paintings. (He's always been promising them to me for Stonyhurst, but I don't think I'll ever get them.) But Paddy continued to be a sort of mystery man and was always a most undependable person. You'd arrange for things to do with him, and he'd never turn up. On occasion he'd just disappear for a long period of time. But we became very close friends, indeed, and I loved him very much.

Though he apparently never had any what I'd call formal education, he nevertheless was amazing in his knowledge. He could quote poetry to you galore and he seemed to have read almost everything. His knowledge of flowers was extraordinary. Again, he was almost infallible on silver. I remember testing him once in the early days because I thought he talked too much about knowing things. We were walking up the High in Oxford and we saw some candlesticks in the window. Paddy remarked that they were lovely pieces, so I asked him what period he thought they were. "Oh, I should think they're about 1712," he said. So I went into the shop and asked the man there, and he said, "They're 1710." So Paddy was right. But still I was always testing him because he had this strange atmosphere about him which sometimes raised skepticism.

As to genealogies, he was a walking encyclopedia. You'd mention somebody as being of a fine family, and he'd say, "No, no, no! You see, their great-, great-, great-grandfather, he married a So-and-So. Oh, no! They're no good at all." Again, of a very well-known English family, he said to me one day, "Notice their wrists. Their great-, great-, great-grandfather was a blacksmith. That's why they're like that." He was amazing. I have a friend who is a member of a rather famous family in England. From time to time he had regaled me with his family history: how they'd become converts, how they had come from a tremendous Irish family, really peers of Ireland. Well, I mentioned this to Paddy Shannon one day, and he replied, "They're nobodies. Nothing at all.

They're only Cromwellian troopers." Some months after that, I was going with a cousin of this friend of mine to some big lunch in the country, and he too spent a lot of time telling me about his medieval ancestry. So I said to myself, "My goodness, Paddy's wrong this time!" When I came back to London I took the opportunity to look up this family in the *Complete Peerage,* which is the most deadly accurate thing and destroys all the dreams and utopian beliefs of families that think they are "somebodies." I found this family of my friend all right, but the *Peerage* said that the original family had died out and that a Cromwellian officer then took on the name. So Paddy was right again! Though one tested and tested him, he usually proved out. He simply belonged to a different world than ours in the matter of knowing families.

In talking about Paddy Shannon I must never forget to mention an extraordinary side to his character—namely, his kindness. I have told you how generous he was with gifts and that sort of thing. But once, he did a really most self-sacrificing thing. For years he had an elderly little housekeeper. Gradually she grew more and more feeble and finally turned into a complete invalid. Well, Paddy spent years taking care of this old lady, nursing her until he himself almost collapsed. He didn't want her to go to a nursing home or hospital, so he became virtually her servant, watching over her, feeding her, tending her. A kind and lovable man.

Inspiring Stories

There are so many people whose memories I like to keep warm. Let me tell you a few stories about some of them.

Evelyn Waugh's wife, Laura, was a Herbert. Her mother was Mary Herbert, a Catholic convert of an Irish family—the Lord de Vesci family—which had a place in Ireland called Abbey Leix. On her mother's side, Mary was of a very old and distinguished family called Wemyss. Scotch, I suppose. Well, Lady de Vesci once told me this story: As a young married woman she lived rather happily on this large estate in Ireland, but she had a great sadness in that she had no children. One day she asked the people on the estate, all her dear Catholics, to pray that she might have a child. And finally, at the age of about forty, while she was in London, she had this child, Mary. When the family came back to Ireland from England, all the people from the estate came out to welcome them home. They took the horses out of the traces and themselves pulled the carriage up to the big house, crying with happiness. Lady de Vesci said to me, "You know, when we reached the great house, I just handed them my child, my little baby. She was their baby, more almost than mine—the baby of their prayers. And I felt then that Mary would someday be a Catholic, because she was the child of all those Catholic prayers." And, sure enough, many years later Mary Herbert did indeed become a Catholic.

Now, when Lady de Vesci was in her seventies, she was still extremely beautiful and very slim. She had been one of the great beauties of the Victorian era. So I said to her one day, "Lady de Vesci, I've always been puzzled how you could possibly have eaten such enormous dinners in the Victorian days. I suppose that you were out hunting all day and came in with a ravenous appetite and then ate your twelve courses." And this slim old lady looked at me with scorn and said, "Not at all, not at all! Whether we went hunting or not, we used to have our twelve courses at lunch and then *sixteen* at dinner." And here she was at seventy-eight or so, still delicate and thin and beautiful.

Lady de Vesci's daughter, Mary, married Auberon Herbert, the younger brother of the Earl of Carnarvon, and that wedding produced an amusing story. In England you have the marriage and then you have got to go round to the sacristy and have the silly little man from the state do the civil ceremony. So when the marriage was over, we all went round to the sacristy, with the four people who were the witnesses or sponsors, Lord Esme Howard, Maurice Baring, Hilaire Belloc, and the most distinguished Sidney Herbert. The young man who was in charge of this civil business called up Lord Howard and asked him to sign his name to the regency. Esme did so, and the young man looked at the signature, decided it wasn't very clearly written and said, "Well, I'd better write it for you myself, hadn't I?" So he wrote in the name just above the signature and then proceeded to do the same for the other three as they each signed. So all four of these distinguished men, Howard, Baring, Belloc and Herbert, were treated as illiterates who were unable to write their own names!

Mary Herbert was always anxious, of course, that her mother should become a Catholic like herself. At her suggestion I did try to approach the question once or twice, but I saw Lady de Vesci withdraw, and so I didn't pursue the matter. Well, when she grew old, she went to live with a great friend of hers near Windsor, about twenty miles outside London. One day Mary came to me and said, "You know, my mother is now in her eighties and she complains that when she's lying in bed, where she spends a good part of each day now, she sees horrible little animals—piglets—crawling about on the walls. It's becoming very disturbing to her." I told Mary, "It sounds like a weakness of old age. Some people, when they get old, become childish and weak, and begin to see things. They can't distinguish between what is real and what is imaginary. It's much like the nightmares of childhood. I don't think there's much to be done about it." Well, about a year later Mary rang me up quite suddenly one day and said, "My dear mother's got double pneumonia, and they don't know whether she will live. I do wish you'd come and see her." So I left Farm Street and went straight out to see Lady de Vesci. When I opened the door and came into her room, there was this lovely old lady, extremely delicate and frail, lying in her bed. Right off she said to me, "Oh, Father, I'm so glad you've come. Will you receive me into the Catholic Church?" So I thereupon did everything that was necessary, and she came into the Church. She lived yet another four or five years until about the age of eighty-nine, I think. But, most remarkable to relate, she never saw those piglets again! That was one of the oddest things I know, the fact that those hallucinations (if that's what they were) should have ceased just at the time she embraced the Faith. But it is a lovely story, isn't it? However, now I'll tell you an even lovelier one.

There is a wonderful old lady (she's about eighty-six now) named Mrs. Helen Plowden. About six years ago a friend of hers said to me, "I want you to meet my beloved friend, Helen Plowden. Do make her a Catholic." So we met and got along splendidly with one another, and eventually she did become a Catholic. She is the most lovely old lady. Her father was a successful painter named Hazeltine. Her brother is also quite distinguished; he lives in Paris and does beautiful bronze horses. She was brought up in Rome in the time of the novelist Marion Crawford and old Mrs. Winthrop Chandler. She married into this very ancient Catholic family and lived in Scotland. Well, she told me that when she was up there in Scotland, miles away from anywhere, one of her children, a most darling little boy, fell and struck his head while at school. When he came home, he complained about not feeling well, so she sent for the local doctor. After examining him, the doctor said, "This is very serious. I'd better send to Edinburgh and get a specialist to come out." So the specialist came out, examined the boy, and said, "I must operate immediately. There's only a fifty-fifty chance, I'm sorry to say." "And so," Mrs. Plowden told me, "I went into another room while they operated. As I sat there praying for my child, suddenly I seemed to see the operating room, with my child lying there on the table. I saw Our Lady, the Mother of God, standing at the top of the table. And she stretched out her blue mantle and took hold of my baby child, and I knew then that he was dead and had gone to heaven. When I finally recovered myself, I went back into the other room and found my baby dead on the operating table." Most extraordinary. Mind you, this was many, many years before she became a Catholic.

I have another story that I think is quite interesting. There was a very remarkable boy up at Oxford some years back, a very brilliant young poet. I had a Catholic friend, now a Benedictine, who was very fond of this boy and hoped that he might become a Catholic since he seemed to be of a very Catholic mind. Well, this Catholic friend wanted to introduce me to this boy, but things happened and I never did meet him. Then my friend came to me with the sad news that the boy had gone to the hospital, apparently very ill indeed of some glandular ailment. Well, I was about to go round to the hospital when I learned that the boy had been removed to a nursing home near Brighton or Bournemouth, some place like that, on the South Coast. So I then wrote to a priest I knew near this private nursing home, asking him to look in on the boy. But the priest wrote back saying that there was no chance of his getting into that nursing home because it was violently anti-Catholic. I recall saying to my Catholic friend even after we received this bad word, "Don't worry, I'm sure everything will go right." Then there appeared in *The London Times* the news of the boy's death. I remember feeling very disheartened and depressed about it. Weeks passed, and one day this Catholic friend brought me a letter and I copied it because I thought it a very remarkable letter. I have it with me and, though it's a bit long, I'd like to read it to you. It's from the nurse who cared for this boy in his last days, and she says:

> I feel sure he was a boy of wonderful intellect. This was evident from his loquacity and clever repartee. But he had great eccentricities of conduct. Before I came, he had a new nurse every day, six night nurses in one week. As soon as he took a dislike to a nurse, she had to go. I believe I was their last hope.
> Never shall I forget the first day with him, and what a difference during the days that followed. His temper was excitable and nervous, together with an ill-balanced, impressionable judgment. He was absolutely full of morbid self-feeling and continually blasphemed and cursed God. At the end of my first day here, to be quite truthful, I was almost hysterical. I sent for the doctor at 9 p.m. He could do nothing with the boy.
> The next morning I went to Mass and I feel somebody prayed hard for him. When I was in church, I felt suddenly I must look after him. I hated doing it, but could not help myself. He did not look up when I entered his room.

But before the end of the day we were great friends. He asked me to forgive him, and to try to be sympathetic. We quarreled daily. When he blasphemed, I just blessed myself. You should have seen the expression on his face when he saw me make the sign of the Cross.

On the day of his death we sent for his parents and asked them if we could send for a clergyman. The clergyman came, but it was dreadful to witness the scene. The boy tried to shout, and when he found his voice had gone, he put his hands over his ears and wouldn't listen. When everyone left the room, I went to him and explained that he was going to die, and it was then too late to send for a priest. He had said he wanted to be a Catholic; so the other nurse, who was also a Catholic, went and got some holy water, and I baptized him and he said an act of contrition. She and I said the prayers for the dying, and he said several prayers after us.

Personally I consider it a glorious death. He clasped the crucifix in his hands and his last words were addressed to you, his Catholic friend, and he touched the relic.

Well, some time after that, Father Woodlock came to me at Farm Street and asked me whether I knew a certain Lady X. I told him I knew of Lady X but did not know her personally. Well, he went on to say she had sent him fifty pounds, which was a considerable sum of money in those days, and had asked him to use it for the poor. And he added that he himself had never even met the lady.

Some time later, the nurse who wrote the letter I just read, and to whom I'd written and had come to know, called to see me. She said, "Oh, I've just been nursing young Lady Y, the child of Lady X." So I said, "Oh, then you may be able to explain the great mystery: why Lady X sent Father

Woodlock a sum of money for the poor." And this nurse said, "Oh, I'll tell you all about that. Lady Y, a girl of about seventeen or eighteen, was out hunting and took a bad fall from a horse. It affected her in a most extraordinary way so that she began to go rigid and then her spine curved and she went into a complete decline. The finest neurologists and other doctors of London were called in, but they didn't know what to do to cure her. I felt I could do something for her without all that trouble, so I just went out to Mass. Later, one morning when I was nursing her, I came back from Mass and met the mother, Lady X, and she said to me, 'Oh, you've been to Mass, haven't you? I'd be so grateful if you'd put up a candle for my daughter next time you're in church and say a prayer for her.' I told Lady X to have done with those superstitious practices, then asked her if she really wanted to do something for her daughter. So I told her to make a great act of love of God and then test her love by making a gift to the poor. Lady X's face lit up and she said, 'I certainly will do that. Whom shall I make the check to? You?' I told her not under any circumstances to make it out to me and put temptation in my way. Suddenly, Father Woodlock's name came to my mind, and I said to make the check out to him at Farm Street. Apparently she did that and, happy to relate, the child recovered in the end." Isn't that interesting? And such a wonderful nurse she must have been, don't you think? She had a splendid sense of the Faith.

Strange Stories

In my time I have heard many strange stories, and I thought you might be interested in hearing a few of them. Some are eerie, some macabre, some sad. Let me start with a rather fantastic one told me by a friend.

Some thirty years or more ago, Abbot Cuthbert Butler of Downside, the man who wrote *The Vatican Council, The Growth of Mysticism* and *Western Mysticism,* happened to be in Dublin when he heard about the death of Lord Gormaston of the Preston family, the oldest Viscountcy in Ireland. Viscount Gormaston having been a Downside boy, the Abbot decided he must go to the funeral. So he got driven out to, I think, Meath in a coach. As they drew near their destination, Abbot Butler heard some strange-sounding barking, so he said to the jarvey, "What's all this barking I hear?" All he got in reply was a shiver from the jarvey—but no answer. Well, he arrived at the place and there was a large gathering at the funeral. In his impeccable but absurdly indiscreet way, he asked the widow, "Lady Gormaston, what is all this barking I keep on hearing?" And she just turned away from him. At that point someone standing by drew him aside and said, "For God's sake, Abbot, don't you know the tradition of the Gormastons? When a Gormaston dies, all the male foxes come out and bark until he is buried."

My friend went on to tell me that his brother asked the Earl of Fingall (the head of the Plunkett family) about it and he said, "Of course, that's true. I was there on that occasion, and as I was going into the chapel, there on the threshold were two male foxes barking."

Now, let me change the theme a bit. The story of Louis XIV's heart is really an extraordinary tale. What I am about to tell you is, apparently, roughly true. I was told it first by a man named O'Malley, who was born and lived at a place about five or six miles outside Oxford near the Harcourt family manor, a beautiful and enormous eighteenth-century house. Well, he told me this story; and then that same cousin of mine who is always right, Paddy Shannon, told me the story, too; then yet a third person reported it to me. It seems that, at the time of the French Revolution, Harcourt was in Paris and somebody said to him, "You know, the Revolution is going to destroy St. Germain des Prés, where the hearts of the kings of France are preserved in little gold cases. You ought to do something about it." So Harcourt went there and somehow managed to get hold of the gold case containing the heart of Louis XIV. Knowing that he would never be able to get the two items through to England together, he took the heart from the case, put the case into the hands of somebody else to get it back to England, and himself took the heart. Now, the heart had become quite tiny—about the size of a large acorn—and, owing to its being preserved in ammonia, was almost like dust. When Harcourt got back to his manor, he sent for an old vicar, who was the rector of a church about twelve miles the other side of Oxford, and was known to be an antiquary. So this nice old clergyman came to dinner at the manor. At the end of dinner Harcourt put the heart across the table and said, "Now, sir, I defy you to tell me what that is." The old gentleman put on his spectacles, examined the heart closely and was very puzzled. Finally he decided to apply a test: he put out his tongue to feel it, and it was so strongly ammoniated that he immediately hiccoughed violently and swallowed the heart! And the heart was so ammoniated and so poisonous that it killed him. He was dead in about an hour. So the heart of Louis XIV of France now lies buried in an Anglican church outside Oxford!

The tone of that reminds me of another tale. I can't vouch for this, but I was told it was absolutely true. It's a bit grim. There was this Italian immigrant who went to the United States and made his fortune. He used to send presents, largely foods, back to his family in Italy. When he died, he provided in his will that all of his goods, possessions and riches should pass to his family in Italy, on condition that he be buried in Italian soil. Well, the lawyer for the estate somehow found it enormously difficult to get the body sent across the ocean (possibly this was during the war). So he finally made a compromise: he had the body cremated, and sent the ashes to Italy with a letter explaining what he had done. Receiving no acknowledgement or reply, some time later he again wrote to the family, telling exactly what he had done, inquiring as to whether the ashes had been received, and explaining that what had been done was in conformity with the conditions of the will. To his horror, the family wrote back saying, "Great heavens! The parcel arrived, and we thought it was some kind of chocolate. So we used it to bake a cake. And it's all gone!" That's a grim Evelyn Waugh-type story, isn't it?

Evelyn, of course, tells such macabre stories that you can't be quite sure that all is exactly right. One of them, which really seems scarcely believable, is about a man who was a heavy drinker. He took so much ragging about the amount of alcohol he had taken into his system that, as a joke, he had tattooed on his chest "Wrap me in ice." Well, then came the Spanish Civil War. Moved by a very generous and high-minded desire to help this socialist cause, he got into a ship to go out to help the anti-Franco people, and en route he developed pneumonia. He was critically ill, feverish, delirious, off his head; so they put him in his bunk. This was a small ship and had no doctor aboard. So when they found written on his chest "Wrap me in ice," they wrapped him in ice! And what with pneumonia, of course, he died. Can you believe that?

Evelyn wrote a short story about a great old lady who was living by herself in solitary splendor when some *parvenus* arrived in the district and began to give big parties. Disgusted at their third-rate way of doing things, she said, "I'll show them how and what to do." She put together her list and wrote out cards of invitation to all the really proper people. When the appointed day arrived, she dressed up to the occasion and came down to her drawing room. But not a soul turned up. And this grand old lady died of a broken heart. When her heirs were going through her belongings after her death, they discovered the invitations all neatly together in a drawer. The dear old thing had forgotten to send the cards out! Well, when Evelyn Waugh published that story, people wrote in and said, "This story has already been told. It was first recounted by Oscar Wilde many years ago." I in turn wrote to Evelyn and asked, "My dear Evelyn, where did you pick up this story? The old lady in it was a great aunt of mine." He wrote back to me, half amused and half angry, and said, "Why, I got it from you, that's where!" Then I remembered that my cousin, Paddy Shannon, had told me the story years before. I must at some time have told Evelyn the story and forgotten about it. Good writer that he was, he noted it and stored it away in his mind.

But now let me tell you one of the saddest of all stories. It was told me by Sir Esme Howard, who heard it when he was in Berlin as an attaché at the English embassy well before the First World War. This was in the days of the glory of the German Army. It seems that the Hussars or one of the other crack military regiments were celebrating at a tremendous dinner at which one of the royal princes was present as guest of honor. During the dinner the colonel of the regiment noticed a wonderful ring on the prince's finger and spoke admiringly of it. The prince said, "Oh, yes, that's a very famous ring. It has an interesting history." After telling this history, he took the ring off his finger to let the colonel examine it, and then it was passed round the table for the other officers to see it. When the dinner had come to an end and they were about to get up, the prince said, "Oh, forgive me, but where is my ring?" And the ring had disappeared. So, as could certainly have happened in the Germany of that day, the colonel said, "Gentlemen, you will all stand up, and everybody is to empty his pockets on the table." Only one officer, very junior, refused to do so. The colonel said to him, "Sir, you know what you must do." Quietly the unfortunate young man left the room, walked out into the garden and shot himself. When they looked through his pockets in search of the ring, they found them filled with what we call sweets—candies, you see. He was one of the very few poor officers in the regiment, and he'd stuffed his pockets with candy for his children but had been ashamed to have to show his fellow officers that he had done so! They discovered the ring later under the table at a spot far removed from the young officer's seat. Apparently someone had knocked it off the table without knowing. It is a terribly sad tale, isn't it?

I think I will conclude this group of strange stories by telling you of a most extraordinary experience I had years and years ago when I was an undergraduate at Oxford. Some Catholic friends told me that there was a most amazing Hindu Christian at New College, a marvelous person. They said that both the Catholics and the Anglicans were anxious to get him and were fighting hard for him. So they asked whether I would be willing to meet him. I replied that I would be delighted, so I went to tea at New College and there I met this Hindu. He had the most marvelous eyes—golden eyes, like those of an eagle or an owl. We talked for some time and finally, sitting there in great tranquility of spirit, he said with the utmost gravity: "They tell me you are a Catholic. Do you really believe that the Holy Trinity is a mystery which cannot be understood?" I replied, "Yes, of course." "To me it's clearer than the daylight," he said. I must say I was flummoxed: Never before or since have I had that kind of reaction to that question.

Postscript

*During the last twenty-five years of his life Father
D'Arcy made almost annual trips to the United States where
he lectured at colleges and universities from coast to coast.
He was greatly admired in this country and developed a host
of American friends. It was our great good fortune to know
him for the last fifteen years of his life. Evenings with him in
our home, and numerous visits with him in London, including several trips to Oxford, were among the most enjoyable
occasions of our lives. This book has been published in an
effort to present sides of Father D'Arcy's personality that no
attendance at his lectures, no study of his books, would dis-
close. We hope that the reader will be as captivated by his
charm and sheer goodness as we were and will be enter-
tained by his lively recollections.*

*Patricia & William S. Abell
Chevy Chase, Maryland*